Informing the legislative debate since 1914

U.S. Farm Income

Randy Schnepf

Specialist in Agricultural Policy

August 29, 2014

Congressional Research Service

7-5700

www.crs.gov

R40152

Summary

According to USDA's Economic Research Service (ERS), national net farm income—a key indicator of U.S. farm well-being—is forecast at $113.2 billion in 2014, down 14% from last year's record $131.3 billion. The 2014 forecast would be the lowest since 2010, but would remain $25 billion above the previous 10-year average.

The forecast for lower net farm income and net cash income is primarily a result of the outlook for lower crop receipts and government payments. In contrast, livestock returns are forecast to be up 15% on the strength of record prices. The 2014 farm bill (Agricultural Act of 2014; P.L. 113-79) eliminated direct payments of nearly $5 billion per year, while market prices for program crops—despite their plunge since late 2013—are expected to remain above trigger levels for most price-contingent programs (peanuts and rice being the exceptions), thus keeping government program support at the level since 1997.

U.S. agricultural exports are forecast to grow in importance for the sector as expanding international economies are expected to lead to continued increases in demand for both higher-quality foods and greater variety of consumer choice in household diets.

In addition to record net farm income, farm wealth is also projected to remain at record levels. Farm asset values—which reflect farm investors' and lenders' expectations about long-term profitability of farm-sector investments—are expected to rise by 2.3% in 2014 to a record $2,906 billion for a fifth consecutive year of gains. However, the outlook for much lower commodity prices in 2014 has slowed the previously rapid growth of farmland values. Farm debt is projected to rise by 2.7% in 2014, thus helping to stabilize the farm debt-to-asset ratio at 10.8%—its lowest level since 2007—for a second consecutive year.

At the farm-household level, average farm household incomes have surged ahead of average U.S. household incomes since the late 1990s. In 2012 (the last year for which comparable data were available), the average farm household income of $108,844 was about 53% higher than the average U.S. household income of $71,274.

These data suggest a strong financial position heading into 2015 for the agricultural sector as a whole relative to the rest of the U.S. economy, but with substantial regional variation. However, declining prices for most major program crops signal tougher times ahead, and considerable uncertainty surrounds producer participation in the new safety net programs of the 2014 farm bill. Eventual 2014 agricultural economic well-being will hinge greatly on the final crop harvests and harvest-time prices, as well as both domestic and international macroeconomic factors, including economic growth and consumer demand.

Contents

Figures

Tables

Contacts

Introduction

The U.S. farm sector is vast and varied. It encompasses production activities related to traditional field crops (such as corn, soybeans, wheat, and cotton) and livestock and poultry products (including meat, dairy, and eggs), as well as fruits, tree nuts, and vegetables. In addition, U.S. agricultural output includes greenhouse and nursery products, forest products, custom work, machine hire, and other farm-related activities. The intensity and economic importance of each of these activities, as well as their underlying market structure and production processes, vary regionally based on the agro-climatic setting, market conditions, and other factors. As a result, farm income and rural economic conditions may vary substantially across the United States.[1] However, this report focuses singularly on aggregate national net farm income and the farm debt-to-asset status as reported by the U.S. Department of Agriculture (USDA).[2]

Annual U.S. net farm income is the single most watched indicator of farm sector well-being, as it captures and reflects the entirety of economic activity across the range of production processes, input expenses, and marketing conditions that have persisted during a specific time period. When national net farm income is reported together with a measure of the national farm debt-to-asset situation, the two summary statistics provide a quick indicator of the economic well-being of the national farm economy.

Measuring Farm Profitability

Two different indicators measure farm profitability: net cash income and net farm income.

Net cash income compares cash receipts to cash expenses. As such, it is a cash flow measure representing the funds that are available to farm operators to meet family living expenses and make debt payments. For example, crops that are produced and harvested but kept in on-farm storage are not counted in net cash income. Farm output must be sold before it is counted as part of the household's cash flow.

Net farm income is a value of production measure, indicating the farm operator's share of the net value added to the national economy within a calendar year, independent of whether it is received in cash or noncash form. As a result, net farm income includes the value of home consumption, changes in inventories, capital replacement, and implicit rent and expenses related to the farm operator's dwelling that are not reflected in cash transactions. Thus, once a crop is grown and harvested it is included in the farm's net income calculation, even if it remains in on-farm storage.

Key Concepts

- Net cash income is generally less variable than net farm income. Farmers can manage the timing of crop and livestock sales and of purchase of inputs to stabilize the variability in their net cash income. For example, farmers can hold crops from large harvests to sell in the forthcoming year, when output may be lower and prices higher.

- Off-farm income and crop insurance subsidies, both of which have increased in importance in recent years, are not included in the calculation of aggregate farm income.

- Off-farm income is included in the discussion of farm income at the household level at the end of this report.

---

[1] For information on state-level farm income, see the "U.S. and State Farm Income and Wealth Statistics," available as part of the Farm Income and Wealth Statistics, Farm Income and Costs, Farm Economy Topics, Economic Research Service (ERS), USDA, at http://www.ers.usda.gov/data-products/farm-income-and-wealth-statistics.aspx.

[2] For a more detailed discussion of the issues in this report, see the Briefing Room "Farm Income and Costs: 2014 Farm Sector Income Forecast," ERS, USDA, at http://www.ers.usda.gov/topics/farm-economy/farm-sector-income-finances/highlights-from-the-2014-farm-income-forecast.aspx.

Figure 1. Annual U.S. Farm Sector Nominal Income, 1960 to 2014F

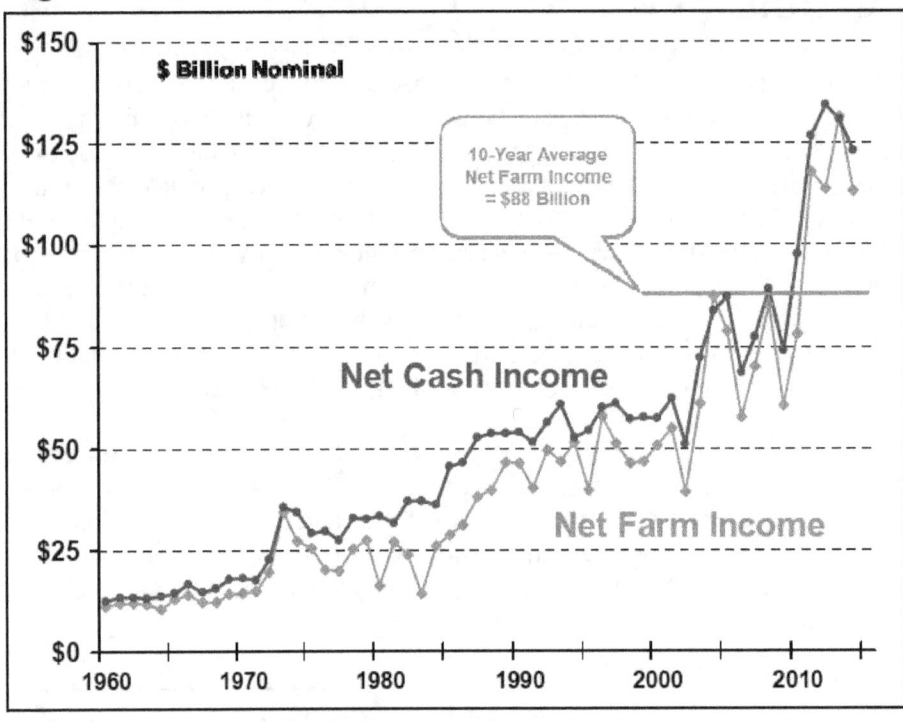

Source: USDA, ERS, "2014 Farm Income Forecast," August 26, 2014. All values are in nominal terms, that is, not adjusted for inflation. 2013 is preliminary, 2014 is forecast.

Figure 2. Annual U.S. Farm Sector Inflation-Adjusted Income, 1960 to 2014F

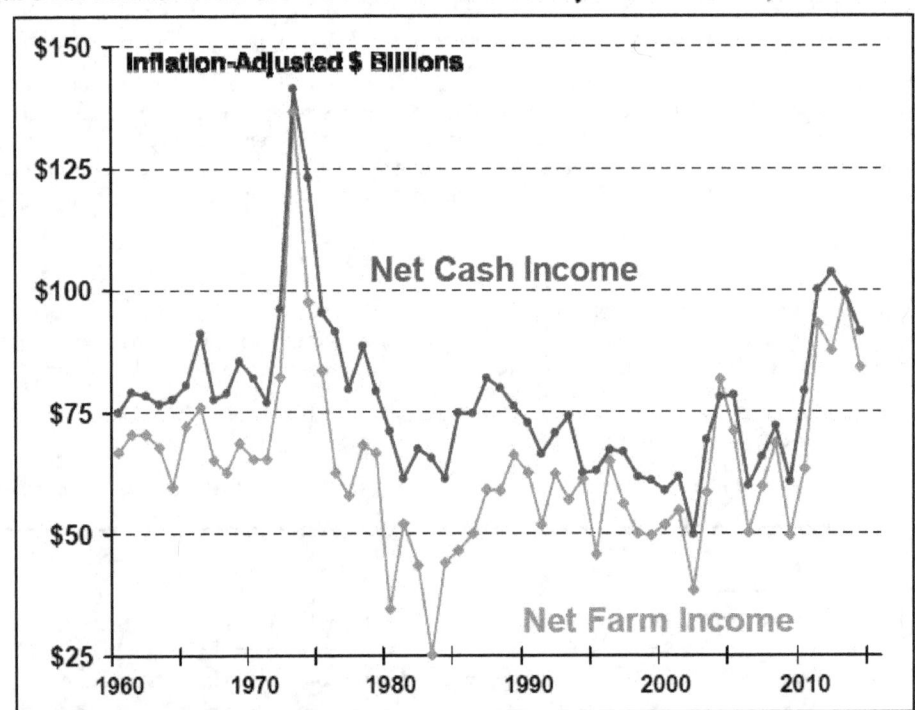

Source: USDA, ERS, "2014 Farm Income Forecast," August 26, 2014. All values are adjusted for inflation using the Bureau of Labor Statistics (BLS), Consumer Price Index (CPI) where 2002-2003=100. 2013 is preliminary, 2014 is forecast.

USDA's 2014 Farm Income Forecast

Both net farm income and net cash income are forecast lower in 2014, primarily as a result of lower crop receipts and government payments. In contrast, livestock returns are forecast to be up sharply on the strength of record high farm prices. The 2014 farm bill (Agricultural Act of 2014; P.L. 113-79) eliminated direct payments of nearly $5 billion per year, while market prices for program crops—despite their plunge since late 2013—are expected to remain above trigger levels for most price-contingent programs, thus keeping government program support at its lowest level since 1997.

U.S. agricultural exports are forecast to continue to grow in importance for the sector as expanding international economies are expected to lead to continued increases in demand for both higher-quality foods and greater variety of consumer choice in household diets.

Total farm asset values are forecast up slightly for a fifth consecutive record high in 2014, while the debt-to-asset ratio is expected to remain at 10.8%, the lowest level since 1960.[3] These data suggest a strong financial position heading into the second half of 2014 for the agricultural sector as a whole relative to the rest of the U.S. economy, but with substantial regional variation.

These forecasts are still preliminary and will depend on the final crop harvests and market developments. The ongoing drought in California remains of particular concern since nearly half of U.S. fruit, vegetable, and tree nut production occurs there. Also, there is some uncertainty about producer participation under the new safety net programs of the 2014 farm bill.

Selected Highlights

- U.S. net farm income is forecast at $113.2 billion in 2014, about $18 billion (14%) below 2013's record (**Figure 1** and **Table 4**).[4] When adjusted for inflation (**Figure 2**), last year's (2013's) net farm income forecast is the highest since 1973.

- Measured in cash terms, net cash income in 2014 is projected lower at $123 billion, down 6% ($8 billion) from the previous year. An estimated $10.3 billion in commodity sales from carryover 2013 end-of-year inventories prevents net cash income from falling as far as net farm income.

- Farm prices for most feedstuffs—feed grains (corn, sorghum, barley, and oats), hay, and protein meals—as well as soybeans have declined sharply through the 2013 harvest and are projected to continue lower in 2014 as U.S. and global grain and oilseed stocks rebuild (**Figure 3** to **Figure 8**).

- Projections based on relatively good growing conditions throughout the major growing zones and only minor decreases in crop planting this past spring are expected to result in substantial production increases (including record corn and soybean harvests), but which fail to offset projected large price declines, thus resulting in lower crop receipts in 2014 (down 7%).

---

[3] See discussion later in the report in the section "Farm Asset Values and Debt."

[4] USDA, ERS, Farm Sector Income & Finances, updated August 26, 2013.

- Record high livestock, dairy, and poultry prices (**Figure 9** to **Figure 14**) result in record cash receipts for animal products (up 15%) that more than offset the declines in crop receipts.

- Despite large declines, commodity prices remain above government support levels, thus shutting off most price-contingent payments. When coupled with the elimination of direct payments by the 2014 farm bill, total government payments in 2014 are projected to fall to $9.3 billion, the lowest level since 1997, the year that direct payments were initiated (**Figure 18**).

- Total production expenses, at $368.4 billion, are projected up 4% in 2014, driven by higher costs for replacement animals (up nearly 23%), plus higher fuel costs (up 6%), and marketing, storage, and transportation costs (up 7%) associated with the expected record crop harvests.

- Record global demand is expected to boost U.S. agricultural product exports to a record-high $152.5 billion in 2014, up 8% from the previous year's record.

- Record farm asset values in 2014 ($2,906 billion), driven by continued strong land values, are expected to exceed increases in farm debt ($314 billion), resulting in a fifth successive record high for farm equity ($2,593 billion) and a debt-to-asset ratio of 10.8%, equal to last year and the lowest since 1960.

Outlook for U.S. Agriculture for 2014

Assuming normal weather conditions prevail in major growing regions through harvest, USDA projects that the 2014/2015 growing period is likely to see a continued rebuilding of global grain and oilseed stocks that began with the large harvests of 2013, thus further moderating crop prices in international markets (**Figure 5** through **Figure 8**). The improving conditions for the livestock sector are evidenced by tracking the evolution of the ratios of livestock output prices to feed costs (**Figure 13** and **Figure 14**), which rose steadily through 2013 and are projected to continue to improve into 2014.[5] However, due to a substantial biological lag in production, the cattle and hog sectors are expected to respond slowly to the improving conditions—that is, delayed supply increases are expected to support relatively high farm prices through 2014 and into early 2015. As a result, retail meat prices in 2014 are projected up 6.5% to 7.5% for beef and pork, and 3% to 4% for poultry.

The two largest U.S. commercial crops—in terms of both value and quantity—are corn and soybeans. These two crops provide important inputs for domestic livestock, poultry, and biofuels sectors. In addition, the United States has traditionally been one of the world's leading exporters of corn, soybeans, and soybean products—vegetable oil and meal. As a result, the outlook for these two crops is critical to both farm sector profitability and regional economic activity across large swaths of the United States, as well as in international markets. Both corn and soybeans are projected to enjoy record harvests (assuming normal weather and trend yields), thus helping to rebuild stocks and pressure prices lower (**Figure 3** and **Figure 4**).[6]

---

[5] Feed costs are generally the largest cost component in livestock operations ranging from 30% to 80% of variable costs. A historical comparison of livestock output prices to feed costs provides an indicator of sector profitability—rising output prices relative to feed costs suggest improving profitability.

[6] USDA, World Agricultural Outlook Board (WAOB), *World Agricultural Supply and Demand Estimates (WASDE)*, August 12, 2014.

USDA highlights four factors as crucial in determining how the U.S. agricultural economy will fair in 2014 and beyond: (1) record global demand, which is expected to boost U.S. agricultural exports; (2) continued strong corn use for ethanol in 2014 with projections of continued growth over the next 10 years, due to relatively cheap corn but strong oil prices; (3) uncertainties surrounding the new farm bill, which will present program choices for most row crop farmers but are expected to have minimal impact on planting decisions; and (4) substantial uncertainty regarding lingering drought in the West, which could continue to affect livestock and specialty crops such as fruits, vegetables, and tree nuts, particularly in California.

Recap of U.S. Agriculture in 2013

U.S. crop production was severely reduced in 2012 due to one of the worst nationwide droughts in several decades. As a result, heading into the 2013 crop year, both corn and soybeans had season-ending stocks projected at or near historic low levels relative to annual usage (**Figure 3** and **Figure 4**). With record-high commodity prices in early 2013 (**Figure 5**), most market watchers anticipated substantial increases in planted acres for both corn and soybeans. However, an exceptionally wet spring across major crop regions of the corn-belt and prairie states resulted in substantial delays in crop planting as well as above-average prevented planting acres. A late-planted crop tends to be more vulnerable to summer heat and dryness and an early frost in the fall, because the normal growing cycle is pushed later into the summer and fall months. Despite the delay in plantings, producers still managed to plant 95.3 million acres of corn, down slightly from 2012 plantings but still the second-most since 1936, and 76.5 million acres of soybeans (equal to average plantings during the preceding five years). As a result, in its preliminary outlook, USDA forecast record 2013 harvests for both crops, assuming normal weather and a return to trend yields.[7] In early summer, this record harvest outlook began to weigh on market prices. By November, USDA projected a record 14 billion bushel corn crop and a near-record soybean crop of 3.3 billion bushels.[8] This outlook pushed both crop prices and feed costs lower—thus simultaneously diminishing the crop revenue outlook while bolstering the livestock sector profitability outlook.

Meanwhile, the high feed costs and lack of forage from severe drought conditions across much of the United States' major crop growing regions during 2012 had resulted in substantial herd liquidation and declining cattle supplies. In early 2013 the dairy, hog, and poultry sectors were also still under extreme financial pressure from high feed costs that had persisted since early 2011. This situation slowly began to unwind during 2013 as crop prospects improved. Record or near-record high meat and dairy products prices coupled with sharply lower prices for their major cost component—feed grains and protein meals (derived primarily from crushing oilseeds)—reversed the severe economic pressure that the U.S. livestock, poultry, and dairy sectors had experienced during 2011 and 2012. Cash receipts for other crops (**Table 2**), including fruits and tree nuts, vegetables and melons, and nursery crops and other horticulture, were also very favorable, generating a combined record cash revenue of $78.3 billion, up nearly 7% from 2012's record.

In short, 2013 was one of the most favorable years ever recorded for U.S. agriculture and represents a very high peak from which the success of 2014 will be judged.

---

[7] WAOB, *WASDE Report,* USDA, May 10, 2013.

[8] WAOB, *WASDE,* USDA, November 8, 2013.

Figure 3. U.S. Corn Stocks-to-Use Share to Rise, Prices to Fall in 2014

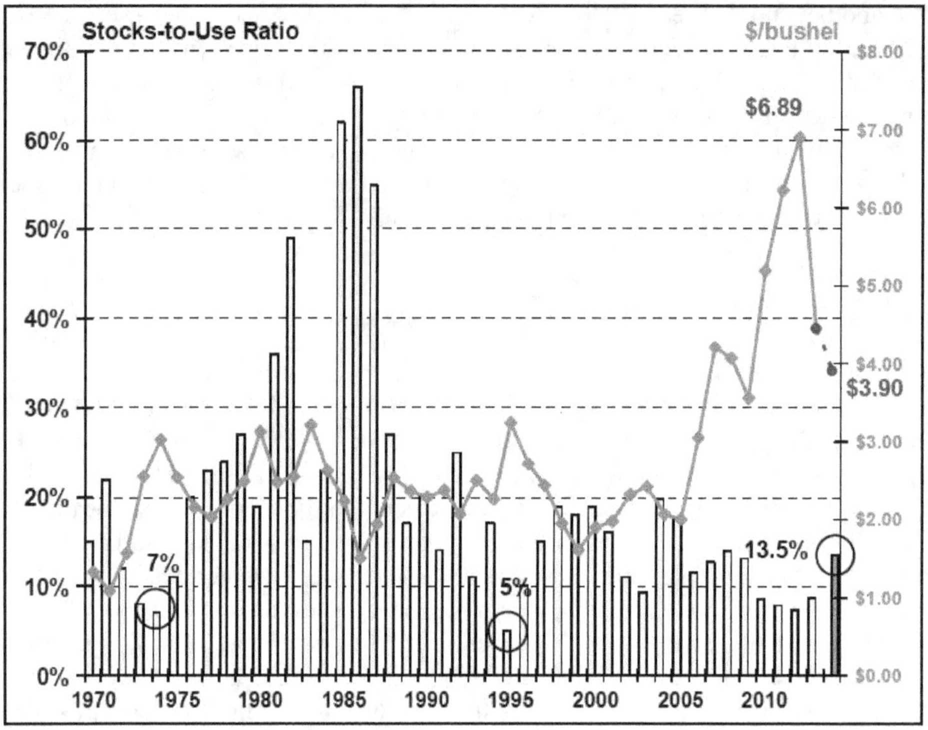

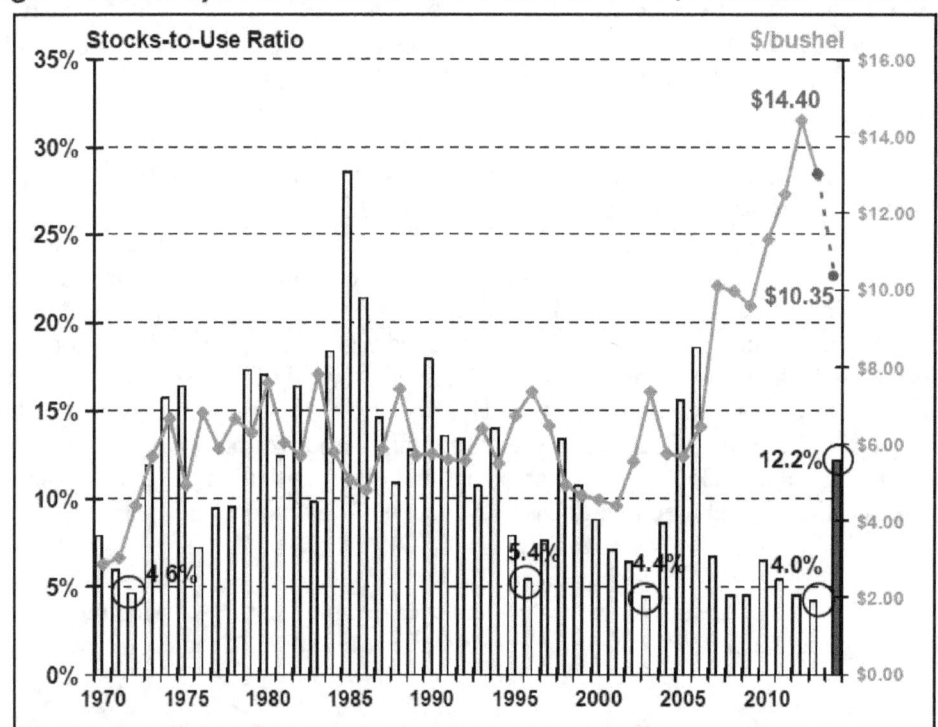

Source: WAOB, USDA, *WASDE*, Aug. 12, 2014.

Figure 4. U.S. Soybean Stocks-to-Use Share to Grow, Prices to Fall in 2014

Source: WAOB, USDA, *WASDE*, Aug. 12, 2014.

Figure 5. Monthly Farm Prices for Corn, Soybeans, and Wheat, Nominal Dollars

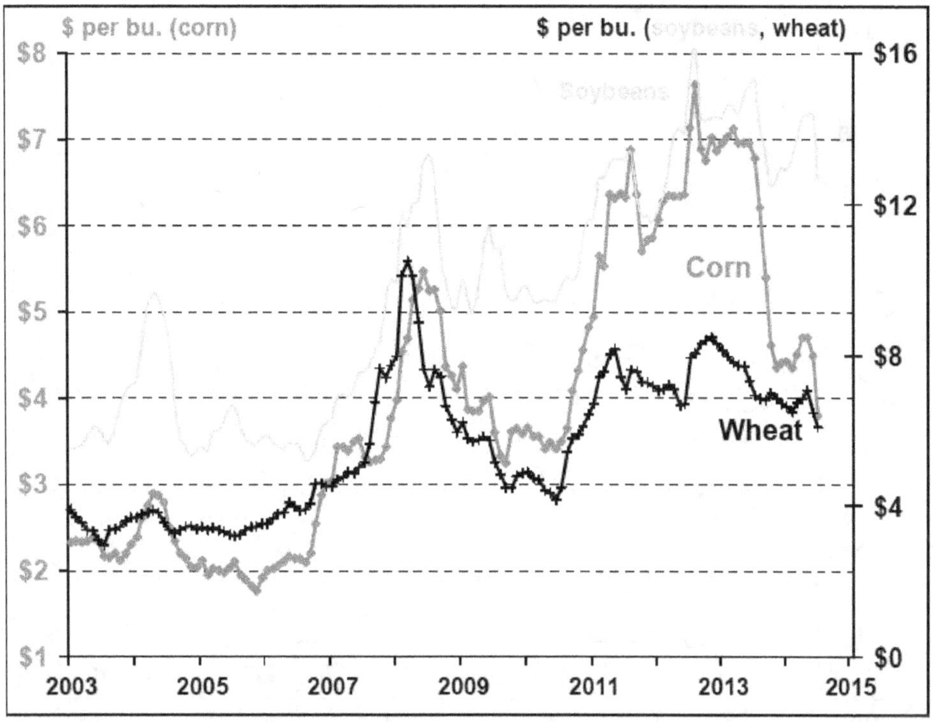

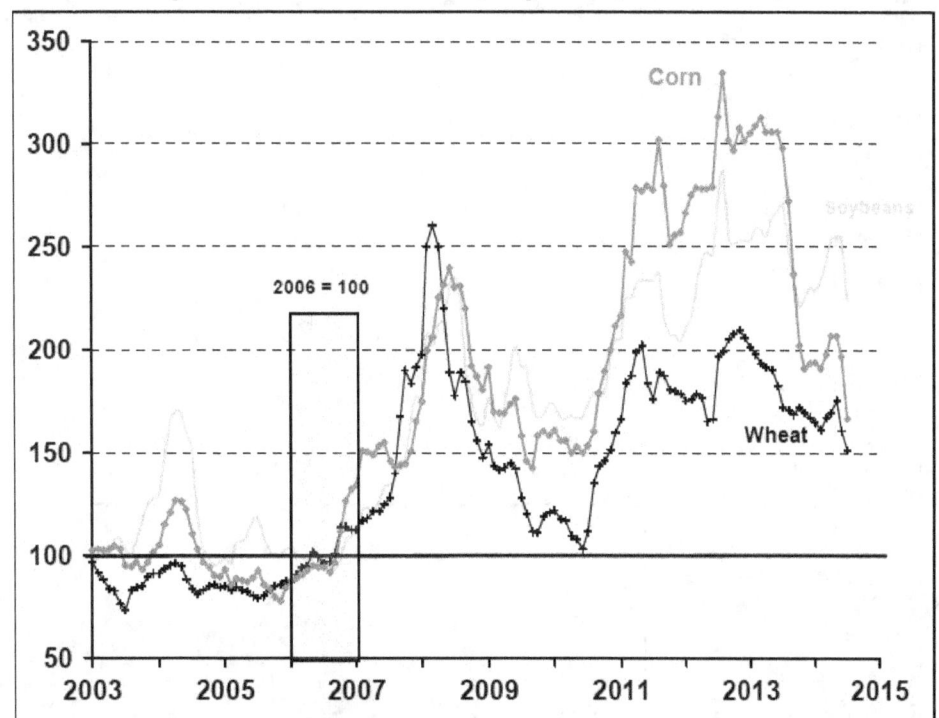

Source: USDA, National Agricultural Statistics Service (NASS), *Agricultural Prices*, July 31, 2014.

Figure 6. Monthly Farm Prices for Corn, Soybeans, and Wheat, Indexed Dollars

Source: USDA, NASS, *Agricultural Prices*, July 31, 2014.

Notes: Prices are indexed to 2002-2003 = 100 to permit relative comparisons.

Figure 7. Monthly Farm Prices for Cotton and Rice, Nominal Dollars

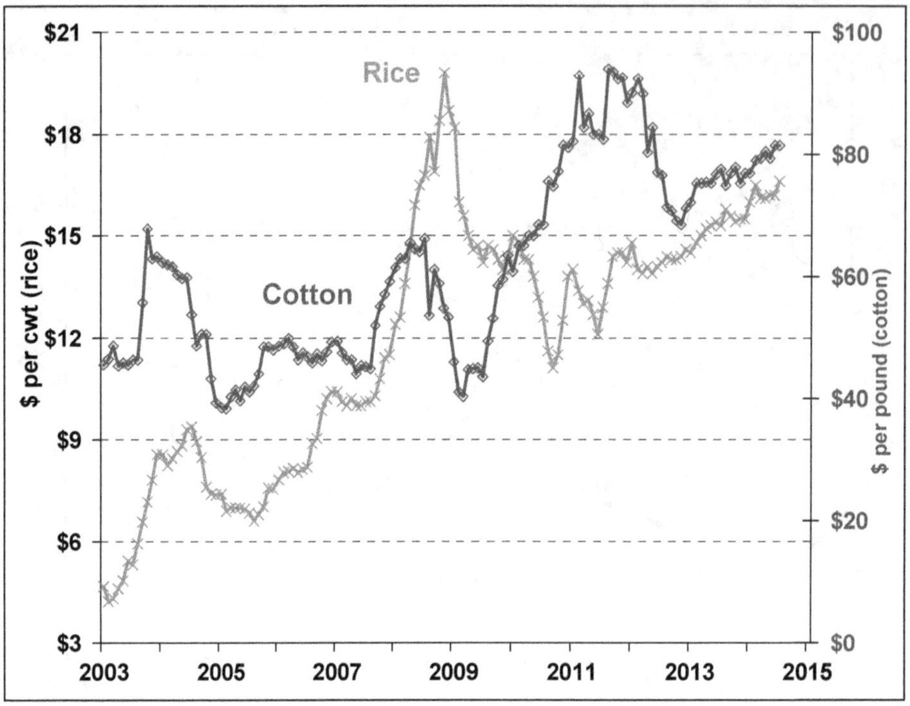

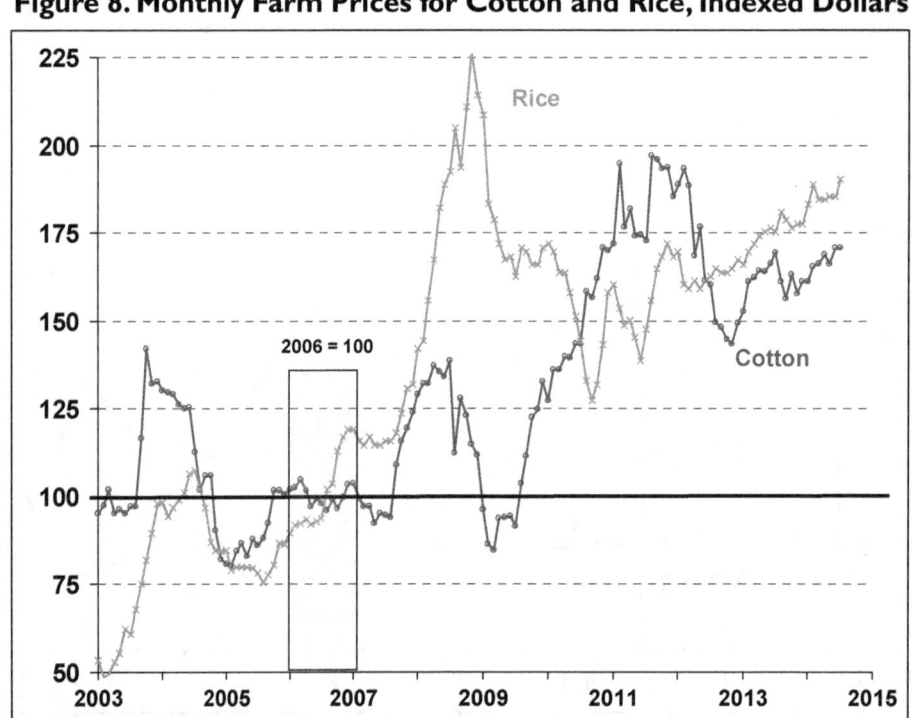

Source: USDA, NASS, *Agricultural Prices*, July 31, 2014.

Notes: cwt = hundredweight or units of 100 lbs.

Figure 8. Monthly Farm Prices for Cotton and Rice, Indexed Dollars

Source: USDA, NASS, *Agricultural Prices*, July 31, 2014.

Notes: Prices are indexed to 2002-2003 = 100 to permit relative comparisons.

Figure 9. Monthly Farm Prices for All-Milk and Cattle (500+ lbs.), Nominal Dollars

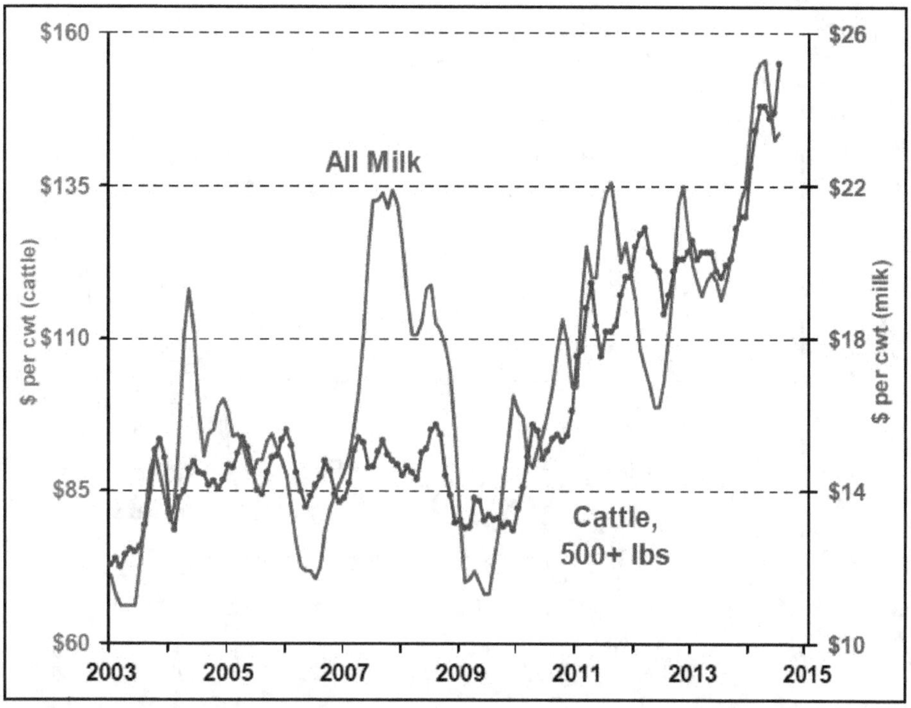

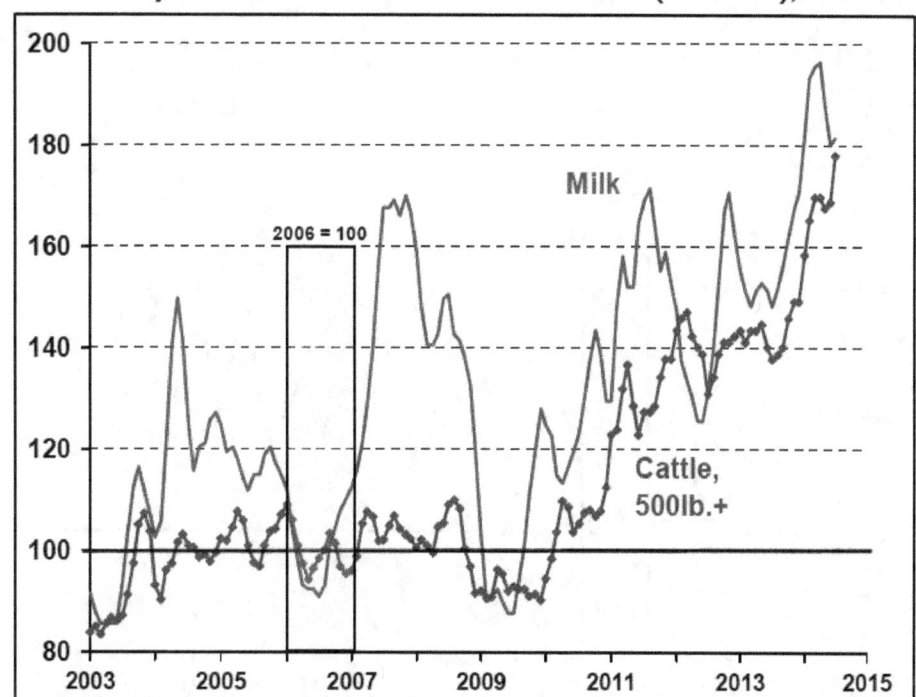

Source: USDA, NASS, *Agricultural Prices*, July 31, 2014.

Notes: cwt = hundredweight or units of 100 lbs; All-Milk averages prices across all classes of milk.

Figure 10. Monthly Farm Prices for All-Milk and Cattle (500+ lbs.), Indexed Dollars

Source: USDA, NASS, *Agricultural Prices* July 31, 2014.

Notes: Prices are indexed to 2006 = 100 to permit relative comparisons.

Figure 11. Monthly Farm Prices for All Hogs and Broilers, Nominal Dollars

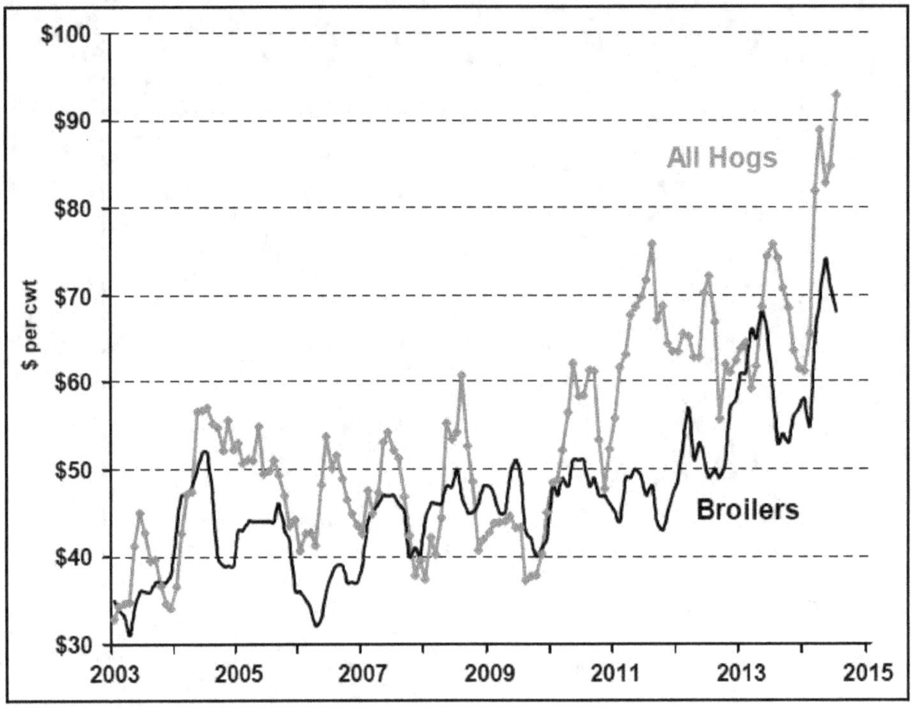

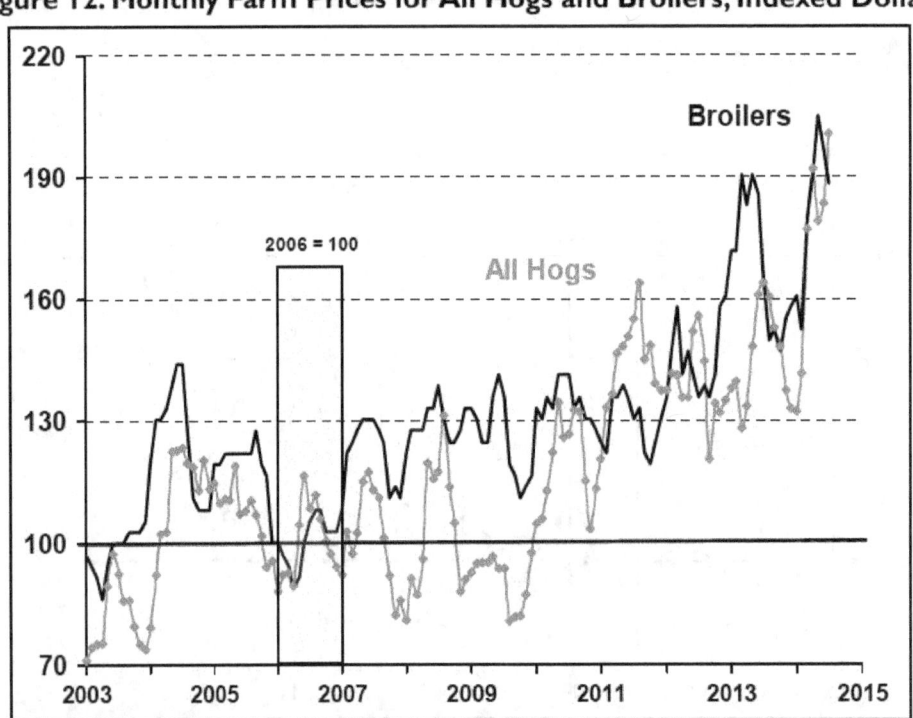

Source: USDA, NASS, *Agricultural Prices*, July 31, 2014.

Notes: cwt = hundredweight or units of 100 lbs.

Figure 12. Monthly Farm Prices for All Hogs and Broilers, Indexed Dollars

Source: USDA, NASS, *Agricultural Prices*, July 31, 2014.

Notes: Prices are indexed to 2006 = 100 to permit relative comparisons.

Figure 13. The Milk-to-Feed Margin Rose to Profitable Levels in 2013

(National average farm-price received of milk less average feed costs per 100 lbs.)

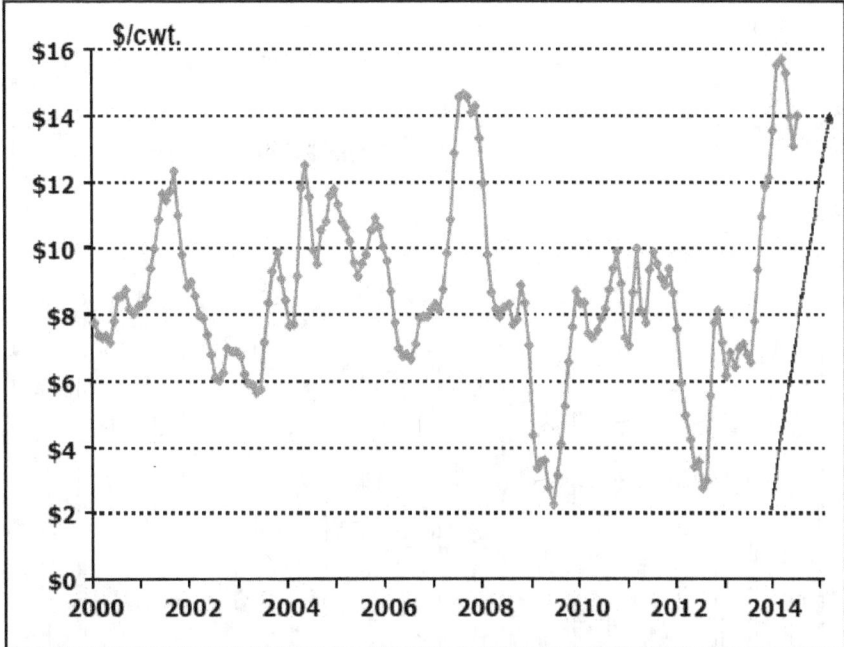

Source: USDA, NASS, *Agricultural Prices*, July 31, 2014; calculations by CRS.

Note: For pricing dairy feed, USDA uses 51% corn, 8% soybeans, and 41% alfalfa.

Figure 14. The Farm-Price-to-Feed Ratios Turned Favorable for Livestock in 2013

(Ratio of national average farm-price received per 100 lbs. of meat to per-unit feed cost)

Source: USDA, NASS, *Agricultural Prices*, July 31, 2014.

Notes: Cattle and hog feed cost is 100% corn; broilers feed cost is 58% corn, 42% soybeans.

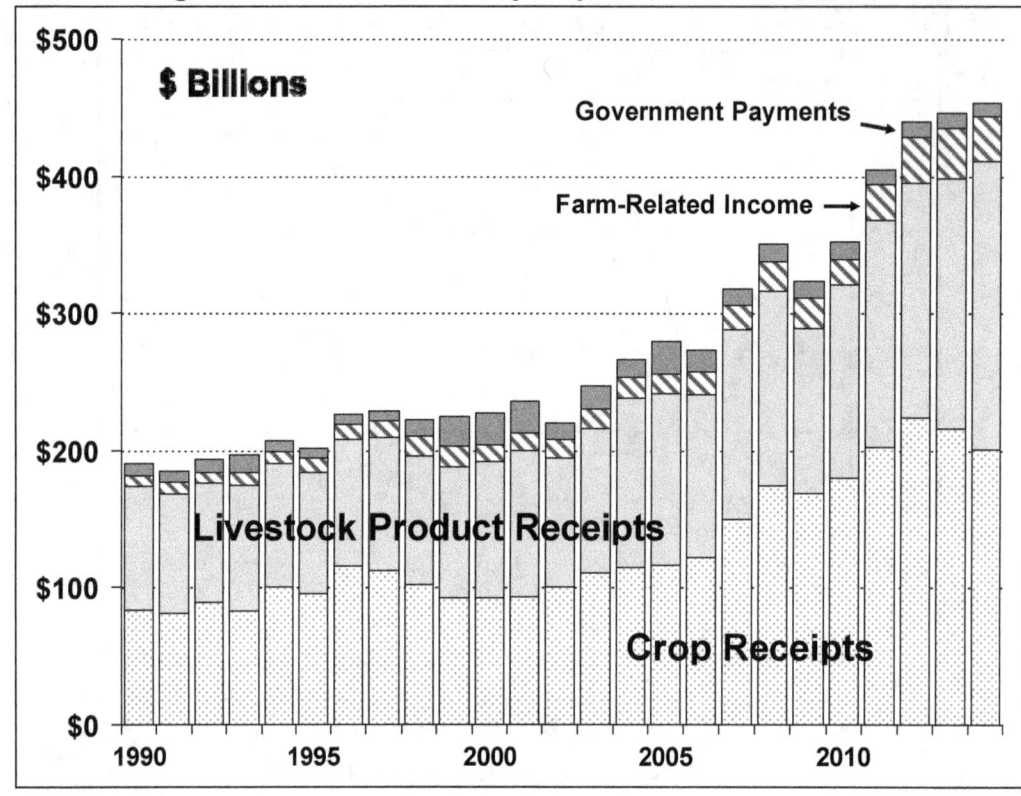

Figure 15. Farm Cash Receipts by Source, 1990 to 2014F

Source: USDA, ERS, "2014 Farm Income Forecast," August 26, 2014.
Notes: 2014 is forecast. Receipts from crop and livestock product sales, and government payments, are described in more detail below. Farm-related income includes income from custom work, machine hire, agritourism, forest product sales, insurance indemnities, and cooperative patronage dividend fees.

2014 Forecast Cash Receipt Highlights

- Total farm sector gross cash receipts for 2014 are projected at a record $451.6 billion, up 1% from last year's record (**Figure 15** and **Table 2**), driven largely by record cash receipts for livestock, dairy, and poultry products.

- Farm sector revenue sources and shares include crop revenues (44% of sector revenues), livestock receipts (46%), government payments (about 2%), and other farm-related income, including crop insurance indemnities, machine hire, and custom work (7%).

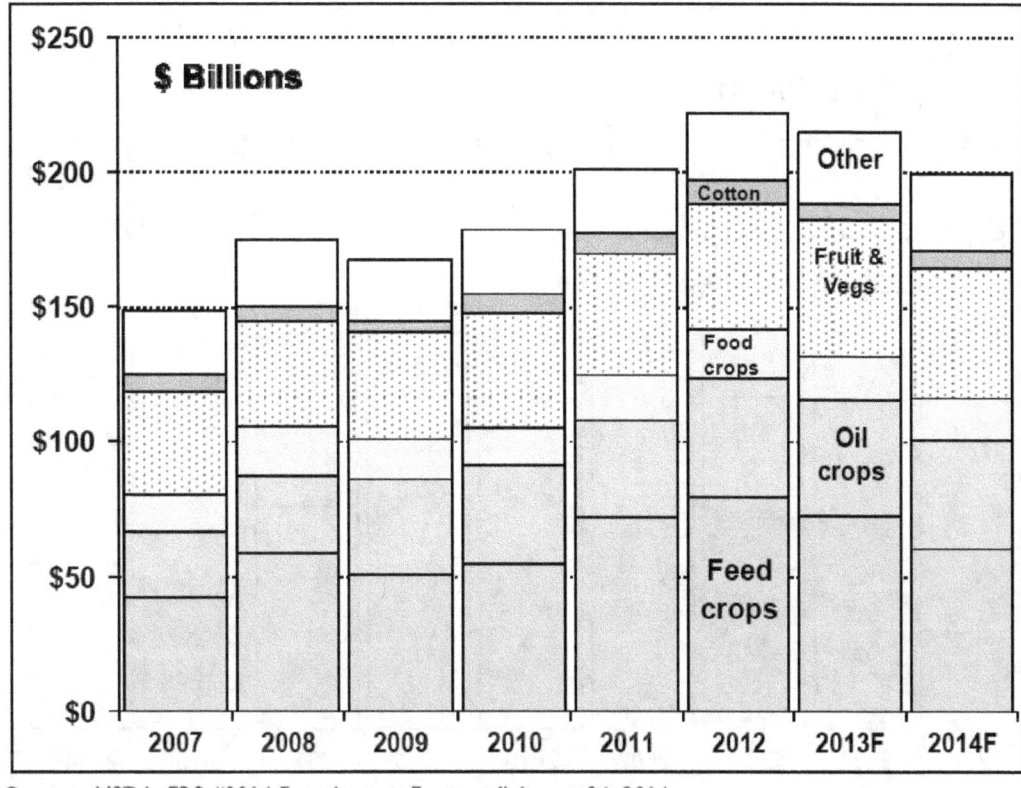

Figure 16. Crop Cash Receipts by Source, 2007 to 2014F

Source: USDA, ERS, "2014 Farm Income Forecast," August 26, 2014.
Notes: 2013 is preliminary, 2014 is forecast. See **Table 2** for details.

Crop Receipts

Total crop sales peaked in 2012 at a record $223.5 billion. In 2014 they are projected down 7.6% year-to-year, at $200.9 billion (**Figure 15**). The crop sector includes projections for:

- feed crops—corn, barley, oats, sorghum, and hay—of $60 billion, down 17%;

- oil crops—soybeans, peanuts, and other minor oilseeds—of $40.5 billion, down 6%;

- food grains—wheat and rice—of $15.7 billion, down 3%;

- fruits and nuts, vegetables, and melons of $48 billion, down a combined 5%;

- cotton of $6.6 billion, up 10%; and

- all other crops including tobacco, sugar, green house, and nursery crops of a record $30 billion, up 7%.

The length and severity of the California drought has important national implications for retail food prices—California accounts for about one-third of U.S. vegetable production, almost two-thirds of U.S. fruit and nut production, about 20% of U.S. milk, and a substantial portion of wine production.

Figure 17. U.S. Livestock Product Cash Receipts by Source, 2007 to 2014F

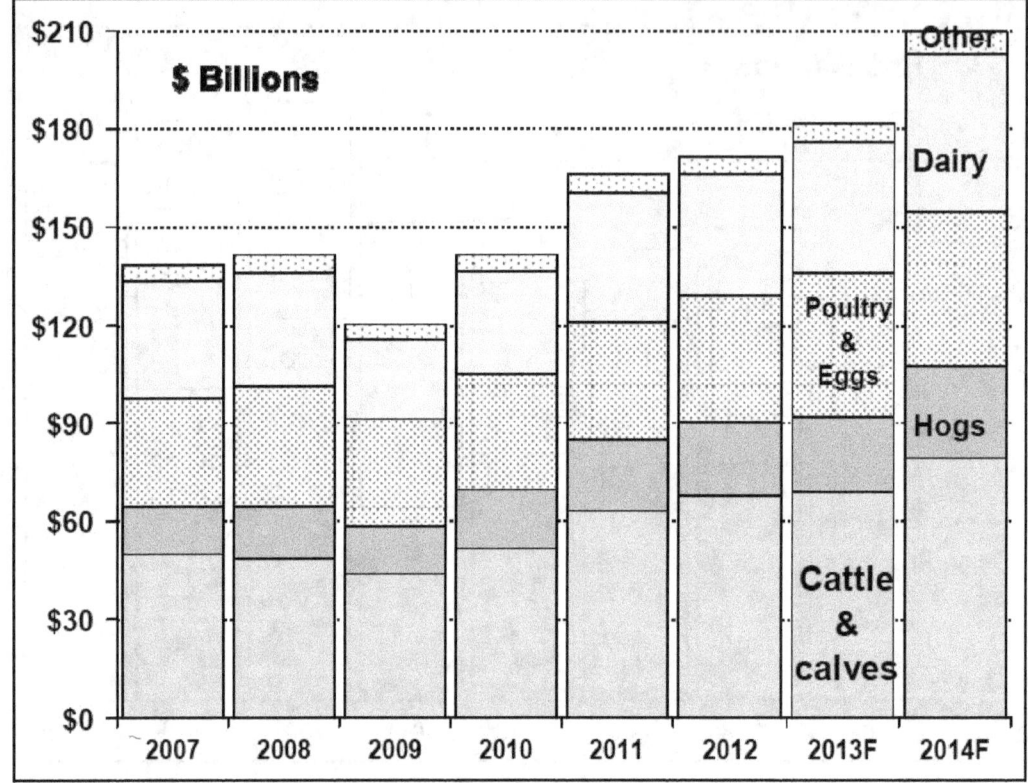

Source: USDA, ERS, "2013 Farm Income Forecast," August 26, 2014.
Notes: 2013 is preliminary, 2014 is forecast. See **Table 2** for details.

Livestock Receipts

The livestock sector, broadly defined, includes cattle, hogs, sheep, poultry and eggs, dairy, and other minor activities. Cash receipts for the livestock sector have grown steadily since the severe downturn of 2009. They are projected record-large in 2014 at $209.6 billion, up about 15% from the previous year's record, driven largely by projected gains in dairy (up 21%), hogs, (up 20%), cattle (up 15%), and eggs (up 14%). Broilers and turkey receipts lag the sector with projected growth of about 7%.

Highlights for individual activities include projections for:

- record cattle and calf sales of over $79.5 billion, up by 15%;

- hog sales of $27.7 billion, up 20% from 2013's record;

- poultry and egg sales of $47.3 billion, up 8% from the previous year's record; and

- record dairy sales, valued at $48.5 billion, up 21% year-to-year.

Figure 18. U.S. Government Farm Support, Direct Outlays, 1997 to 2014F

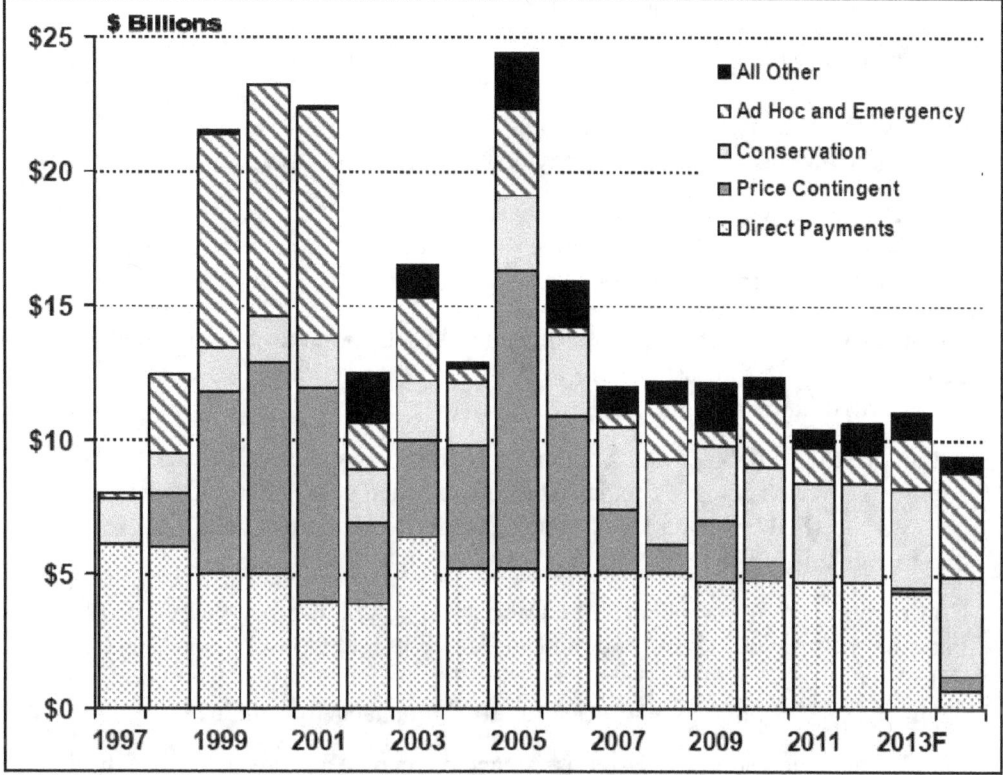

Source: USDA, ERS, "2014 Farm Income Forecast," August 26, 2014.

Notes: Data are on a fiscal year basis and may not correspond exactly with the crop or calendar year; 2013 is preliminary, 2014 is forecast. Direct payments include production flexibility contract payments enacted under the 1996 farm bill and fixed direct payments of the 2002 and 2008 farm bills; price-contingent outlays include loan deficiency payments, marketing loan gains, counter-cyclical payments and ACRE payments; conservation outlays include Conservation Reserve Program payments along with other conservation program outlays; Ad Hoc and Emergency includes emergency supplemental crop and livestock disaster payments and market loss assistance payments for relief of low commodity prices; and "All Other" outlays include peanut quota buyout payments, milk income loss payments, tobacco transition payments, and other miscellaneous expenditures.

Government Payments

Government farm payments are projected lower in 2014 at $9.3 billion (down 15%). This would be the lowest outlay since 1997. The decline is due almost entirely to the elimination of annual direct payments of about $5 billion. In addition, relatively high commodity prices (above government program payment triggers) are expected to keep payments under the price-contingent programs at minimal levels for all but a few commodities—namely, rice and peanuts (**Figure 18**).

- Government payments are expected to represent a relatively small share (2%) of projected gross cash income of $451 billion (**Figure 15**).

- In contrast, government payments are expected to represent 8% of net farm income of $113.2 billion; however, the importance of government payments as a percent of net farm income varies nationally by sector and region.

- Farm fixed direct payments, whose payment rates were fixed in previous legislation, are eliminated by the 2014 farm bill.[9]

- Cotton producers are eligible to receive transition payments (new under the 2014 farm bill) for crop years 2014 and 2015 as they transition into coverage authorized by the new Stacked Income Protection Plan (STAX).[10] Fixed by legislation, these cotton transition payments are forecast at $650 million in 2014.

- Payments under the price-contingent marketing loan benefit are forecast at $180 million in 2014, as program crop prices are expected to remain above most program payment triggers—the exception being rice and peanuts (**Table 7**).

- Payments under the Average Crop Revenue (ACRE) program for 2013 that will go out in 2014 are forecast at $315 million, mostly for corn and soybeans that were hardest hit by drought.

- Although still available in 2014, almost no Milk Income Loss Contract payments—which compensate dairy producers when domestic milk prices fall below a specified benchmark price subject to feed-cost adjustments—are forecast due to high milk prices and relatively low feed costs.

- Conservation programs include all conservation programs operated by USDA's Farm Service Agency (FSA) and the Natural Resources Conservation Service (NRCS) that provide direct payments to producers. Estimated conservation payments of $3.7 billion are forecast for 2014, unchanged from 2013.

- Supplemental and ad-hoc disaster assistance payments are forecast at $3.9 billion in 2014, a 100% increase from 2013 levels. The continuing drought in California and the southern Plains is expected to increase payouts, especially from the Livestock Forage Program (LFP).[11] Livestock producers are eligible to receive payments under the Livestock Forage Program (LFP) and the Livestock Indemnity Program (LIP) retroactive to FY2012. Payments under these two programs are for multiple years, mostly covering losses (feed expenses) incurred during the 2012 drought. Some Noninsured Assistance Program payments also are expected to be made to livestock and specialty crop producers for whom no commodity insurance program is available.

---

[9] For details see CRS Report R43076, *The 2014 Farm Bill (P.L. 113-79): Summary and Side-by-Side.*

[10] Ibid.

[11] CRS Report RS21212, *Agricultural Disaster Assistance.*

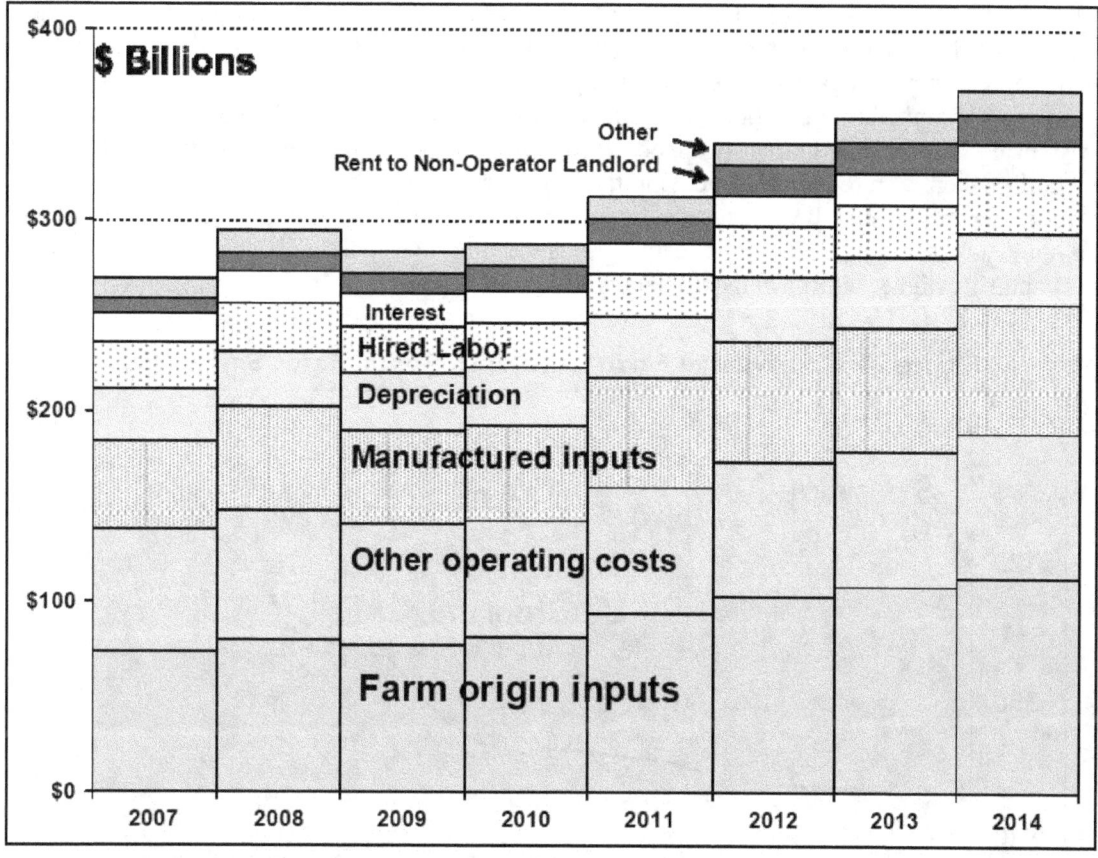

Figure 19. Farm Production Expenses by Source, 2007 to 2014F

Source: USDA, ERS, "2014 Farm Income Forecast," August 26, 2014.

Notes: 2013 is preliminary, 2014 is forecast. See **Table 3** for details. "Other operating costs" includes crop insurance premiums, contract labor, machine hire and custom work, marketing, storage, and transportation, and repair and maintenance. "Other" includes property taxes, noncash labor perquisites, and miscellaneous cost items.

Production Expenses

Production expenses for 2014 for the U.S. agricultural sector are projected up 4% at $368 billion (**Figure 19** and **Table 3**). The increase in expenses will affect crop and livestock farms differently.

- The principal expenses for livestock farms—that is, feed and feeder animals and poultry—are expected to move in opposite directions, as feed costs decline by about 3% while replacement animal costs rise by nearly 23%. In the net, principal livestock expenses are forecast up 4% from 2013 at $90 billion.

- In contrast, the principal crop expenses—that is, seed, fertilizer, pesticides, and crop insurance premiums—are forecast up by nearly 5% to $104 billion. The miscellaneous operating expenses category (**Table 3**), which is projected up $2.5 billion (+7%) to $36.9 billion, includes crop insurance premiums and thus directly impacts crop production.

Cash rental rates—which were set the preceding fall of 2013 or in early spring of 2014—still reflect the high prices and large net returns of the preceding several years and have yet to decline (**Figure 20**). Total net rent to non-operator landlords is projected down about 6% due to the decrease in corn plantings. However, the high per-acre cash rental rates may cause a pinch in cash-flow for some farm operations, especially those that did not forward contract any sales in early spring before market prices dropped off to current levels. Some landlords may be forced to renegotiate their cash rental agreements in the fall after harvest. Those grain farmers with livestock operations may be able to benefit from record or near-record high prices for cattle, hogs, and poultry by using the relatively cheaper grains to fatten livestock herds and poultry flocks, thus capturing higher returns in the associated livestock markets.

Figure 20. U.S. Average Farm Land Cash Rental Rates Since 1999

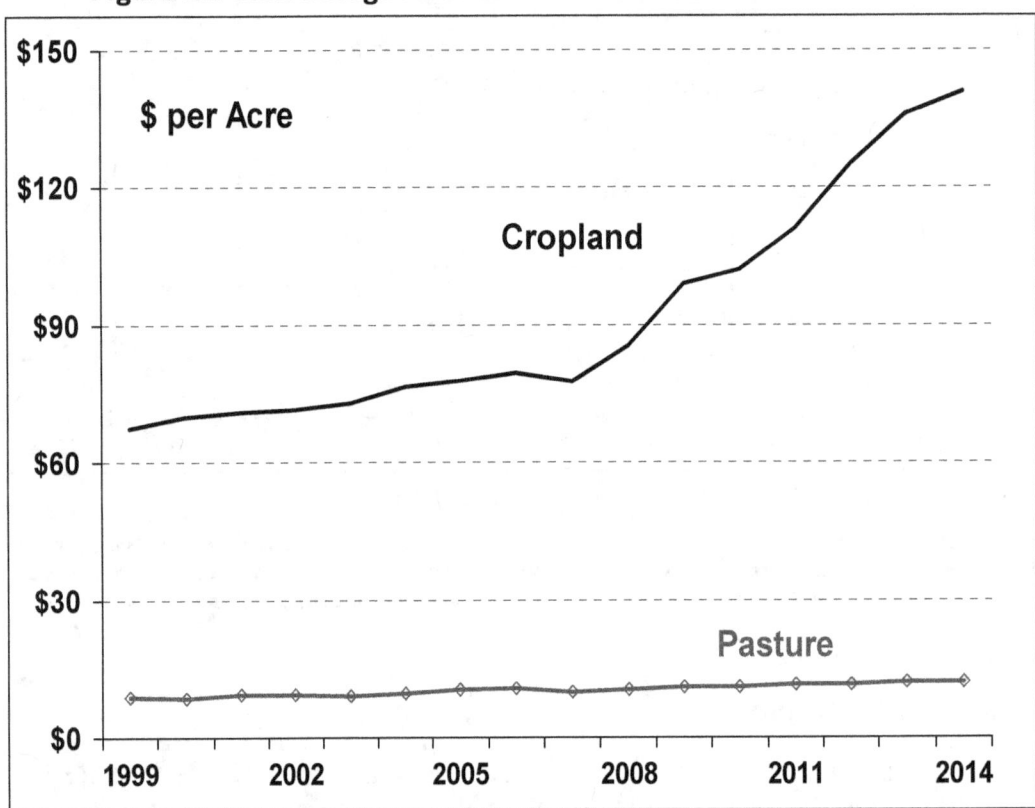

Source: USDA, NASS, "Quick Stats," downloaded August 25, 2014.

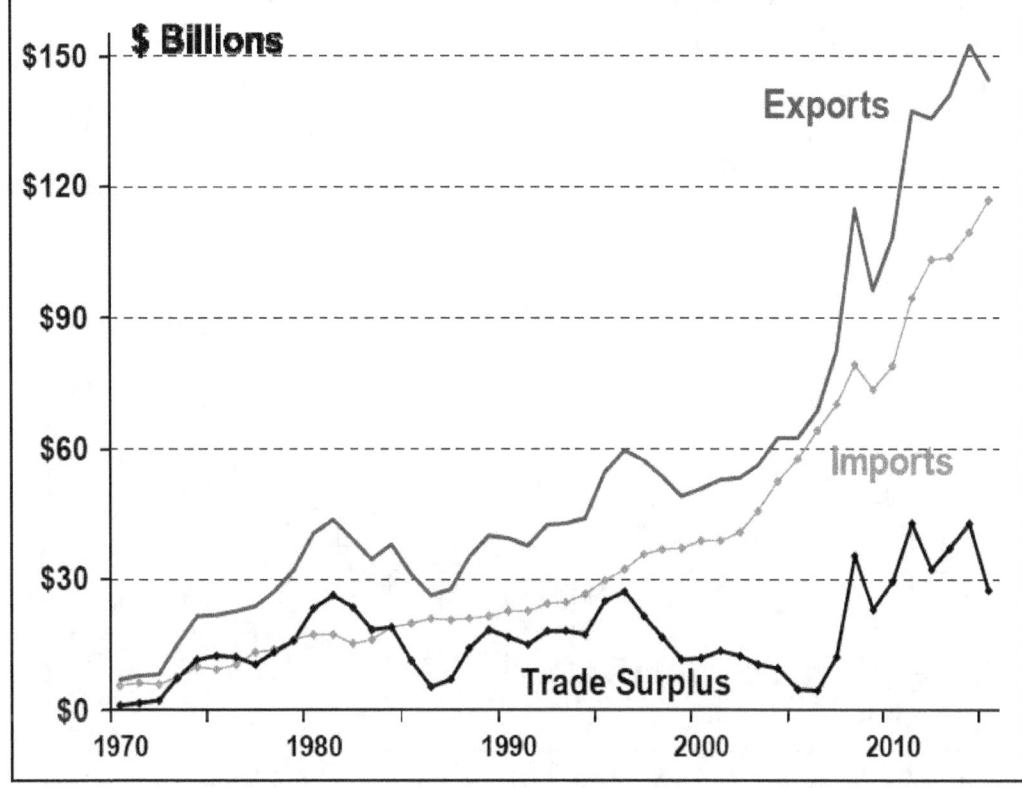

Figure 21. U.S. Agricultural Trade Since 1970

Source: USDA, Outlook for U.S. Agricultural Trade, AES-83, August 28, 2014, ERS, USDA.

Notes: 2013 is an estimate, 2014 is a projection.

Agricultural Trade Outlook

A major catalyst behind projections for stronger farm income is the strength of U.S. agricultural exports, forecast at a record $152.5 billion in 2014, up 8% from 2013's previous record (**Figure 21**). U.S. agricultural imports also are projected record-large in 2014 at $109.5 billion, up 5% year-to-year. The resulting U.S. agricultural trade surplus is projected at $43 billion in 2014, up 16%.

- The top three markets for U.S. agricultural exports are China, Canada, and Mexico, where imports from the United States have surged by about $31 billion since 2009 to a combined projection of $72.5 billion in FY2014 (**Figure 22**).

- A substantial portion of the increase in U.S. agricultural exports since 2010 has also been due to higher-priced grain and feed shipments plus record oilseed exports to China, and growing animal product exports to East Asia.[12]

- The fourth- and fifth-largest U.S. export markets are Japan and the EU, which are projected to account for $25.6 billion in imports in FY2014. Although important as major buyers of U.S. agricultural products, these two markets have shown relatively limited growth when compared with the rest of the world.

---

[12] USDA, ERS, *Outlook for U.S. Agricultural Trade*, AES-83, August 28, 2014, ERS, USDA.

Figure 22. U.S. Agricultural Exports Have Surged Higher Since 2006 Driven by China, NAFTA partners (Canada & Mexico), and Developing Countries

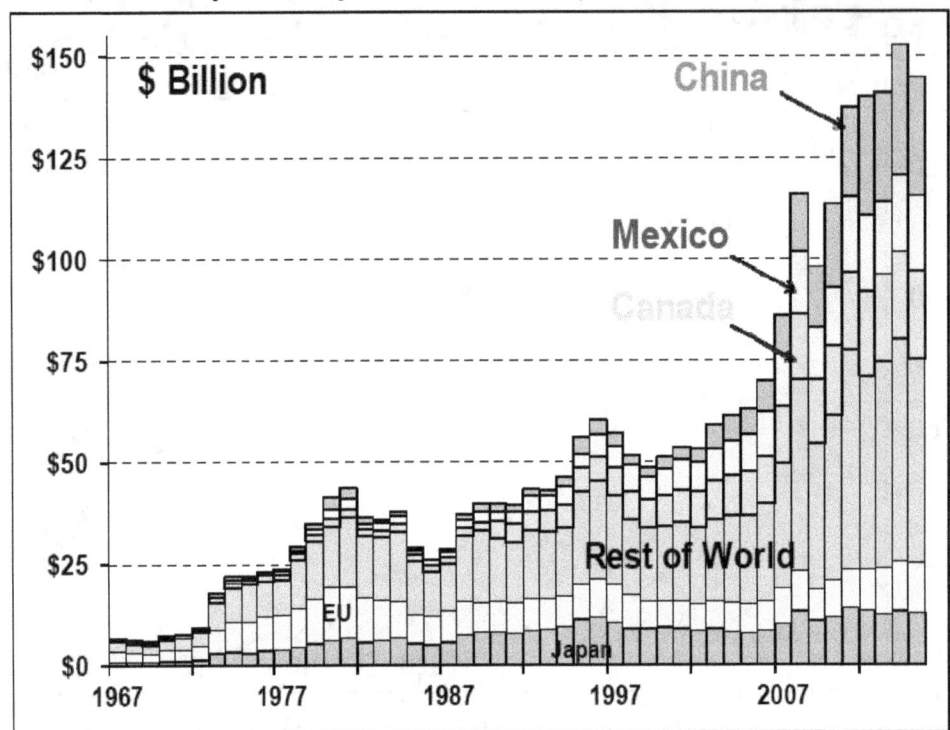

Source: USDA, *Outlook for U.S. Agricultural Trade*, AES-83, August 28, 2014, ERS, USDA.

- The "Rest of World" component of U.S. trade includes Middle Eastern, African, and Southeast Asian markets that have shown dramatic import growth of U.S. agricultural products in recent years—growing by $19 billion (52%) since 2009.

- As a share of total gross farm receipts, U.S. agricultural exports are projected to account for 32% of earnings in 2014 (**Figure 24**).

- In 2015, the early outlook is for a slight fallback in exports to $144.5 billion, still the second-highest total on record.

- Over the past four decades, steady growth in high-valued export products (**Figure 23**) has helped to push U.S. agricultural export value to ever higher totals. This pattern plateaued temporarily in 2006, when rapid growth in demand from both international commodity markets and domestic biofuels pushed prices for most bulk crops (especially feed grains and oilseeds) to record levels. As grain and oilseed prices recede, so will the bulk value share of U.S. exports.

- Bulk commodity shipments (primarily wheat, rice, feed grains, soybeans, cotton, and unmanufactured tobacco) are forecast at a record low 31% share of total U.S. agricultural exports in 2015, at $44.2 billion.

- In contrast, high-valued export products—including horticultural, livestock, poultry, and dairy—are forecast at $100.3 billion in 2015.

Figure 23. U.S. Agricultural Trade: Bulk vs. High-Value Shares

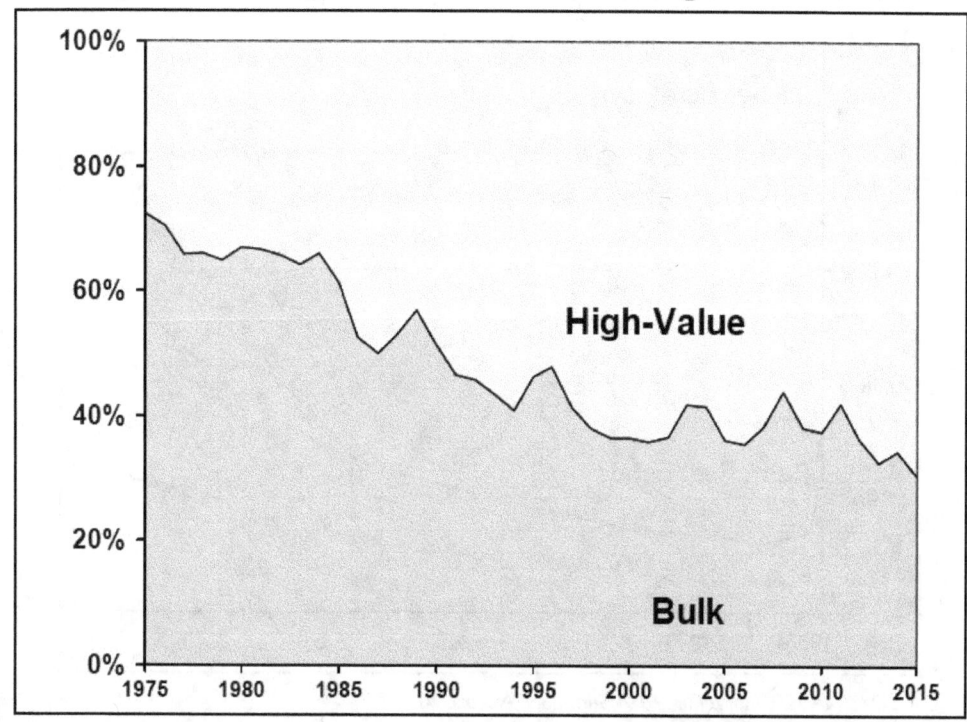

Source: USDA, *Outlook for U.S. Agricultural Trade*, AES-83, August 28, 2014, ERS, USDA.

Figure 24. U.S. Agricultural Export Value as Share of Gross Cash Income

Source: USDA, *Outlook for U.S. Agricultural Trade*, AES-83, August 28, 2014, ERS, USDA.

Figure 25. U.S. Average Farm Land Values, 1985 to 2014F

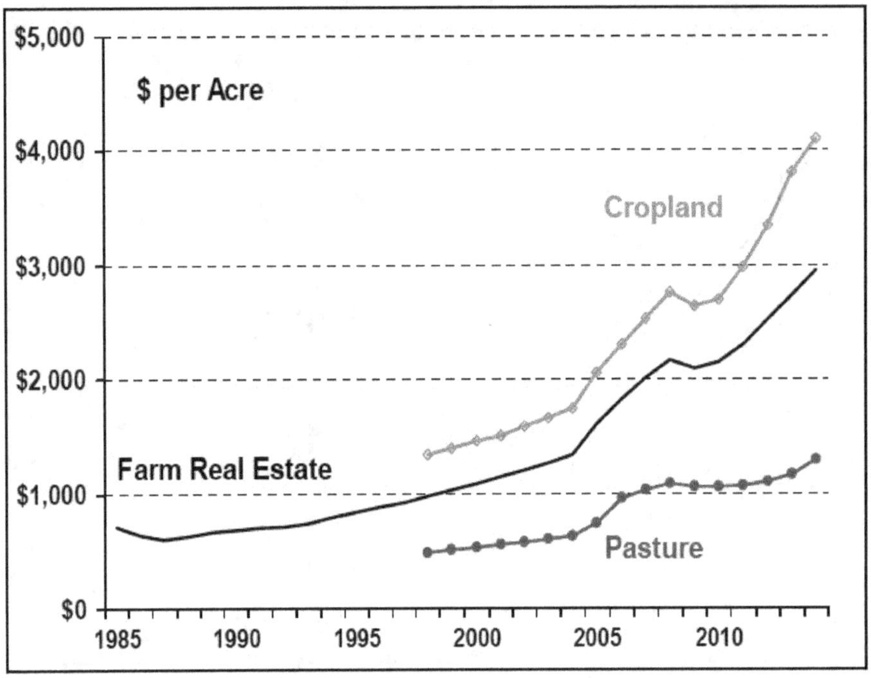

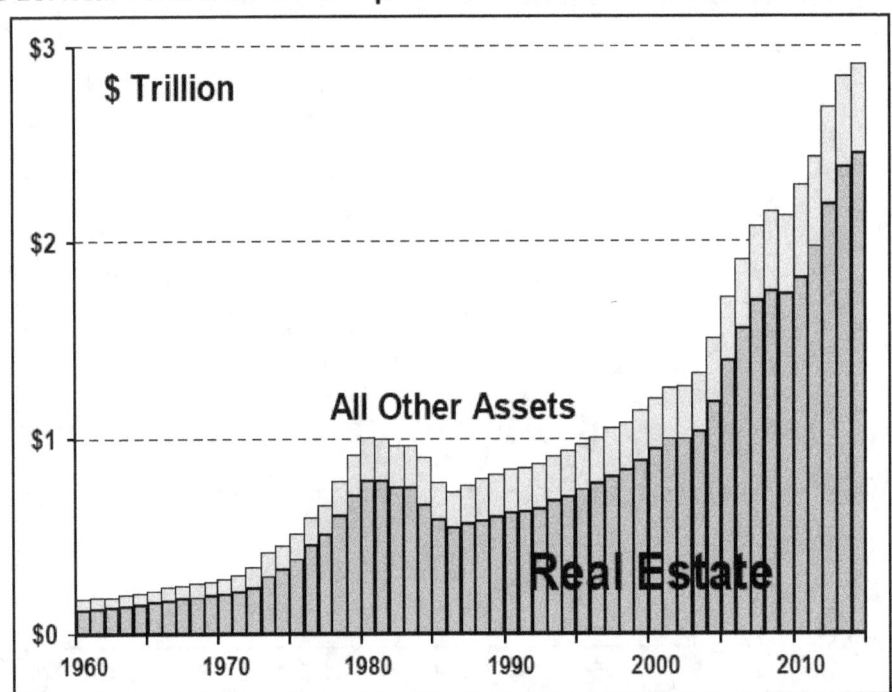

Source: USDA, NASS, *Land Values 2014 Summary*, August 2014.

Notes: 2014 is a forecast. Farm real estate value measures the value of all land and buildings on farms. Cropland and pasture values are only available since 1998.

Figure 26. Real Estate Assets Comprise 84% of Total Farm Sector Assets in 2014

Source: USDA, ERS, "2014 Farm Income Forecast," August 26, 2014; 2014 is forecast.

Notes: Non-real estate assets include financial assets, inventories of agricultural products, and the value of machinery and motor vehicles.

Farm Asset Values and Debt

The U.S. farm income and asset-value situation and outlook suggest a strong financial position heading into 2015 for the agriculture sector as a whole.

Measuring Farm Wealth

A useful measure of the farm sector's financial wherewithal is farm sector net worth as measured by farm assets minus farm debt. A summary statistic that captures this relationship is the debt-to-asset ratio.

Farm Assets include both physical and financial farm assets. **Physical Assets** include land and buildings, farm equipment, on-farm inventories of crops and livestock, and other miscellaneous farm assets. **Financial Assets** include cash, bank accounts, and investments such as stocks and bonds.

Farm Debt includes both business and consumer debt linked to real estate and non-real estate assets of the farm sector.

The **Debt-to-Asset Ratio** compares the farm sector's outstanding debt related to farm operations relative to the value of the sector's aggregate assets. Change in the debt-to-asset ratio is a critical barometer of the farm sector's financial performance with lower values indicating greater financial resiliency. A smaller debt-to-asset ratio suggests that the sector is better able to withstand short-term increases in debt related to interest rate fluctuations or changes in the revenue stream related to lower output prices, higher input prices, or production shortfalls.

The largest single component in a typical farmer's investment portfolio is their farmland. As a result, real estate values affect the financial well-being of agricultural producers and serve as the principal source of collateral for farm loans.

- Farm asset values—which reflect farm investors' and lenders' expectations about long-term profitability of farm sector investments—are projected up 2.3% in 2014 to $2,906 billion, reflecting a continued strong outlook in the general farm economy (**Table 6**).

- Higher farm asset values are due primarily to stronger farm real estate values (**Figure 25** and **Figure 26**). Real estate traditionally accounts for the bulk of total value of farm sector assets.

- After rebounding from a 1% decline during 2009—the first decline since 1986—farm real estate values have grown by an estimated 36%, due largely to strong crop prices. In 2014, real estate assets are expected to account for 84% of total farm assets.

- Land value growth is closely linked to commodity prices and is expected to plateau or recede slightly if the forecasts for lower commodity prices and the prospect for continued global stock recovery for grains and oilseeds are realized in 2014 and beyond.

- Meanwhile, total farm debt is forecast to rise to $313.5 billion in 2014 (up 2.7%).

- Farm equity (or net worth, defined as asset value minus debt) is projected record-high in 2014, at $2,593 billion.

- The farm debt-to-asset ratio had been steadily declining since 1985's peak value of 23%—except for a one-year reversal in 2002 and a two-year reversal in 2008 and 2009—to 10.8% in 2014 (**Figure 27**).

Figure 27. U.S. Farm Debt-to-Asset Ratio Since 1960

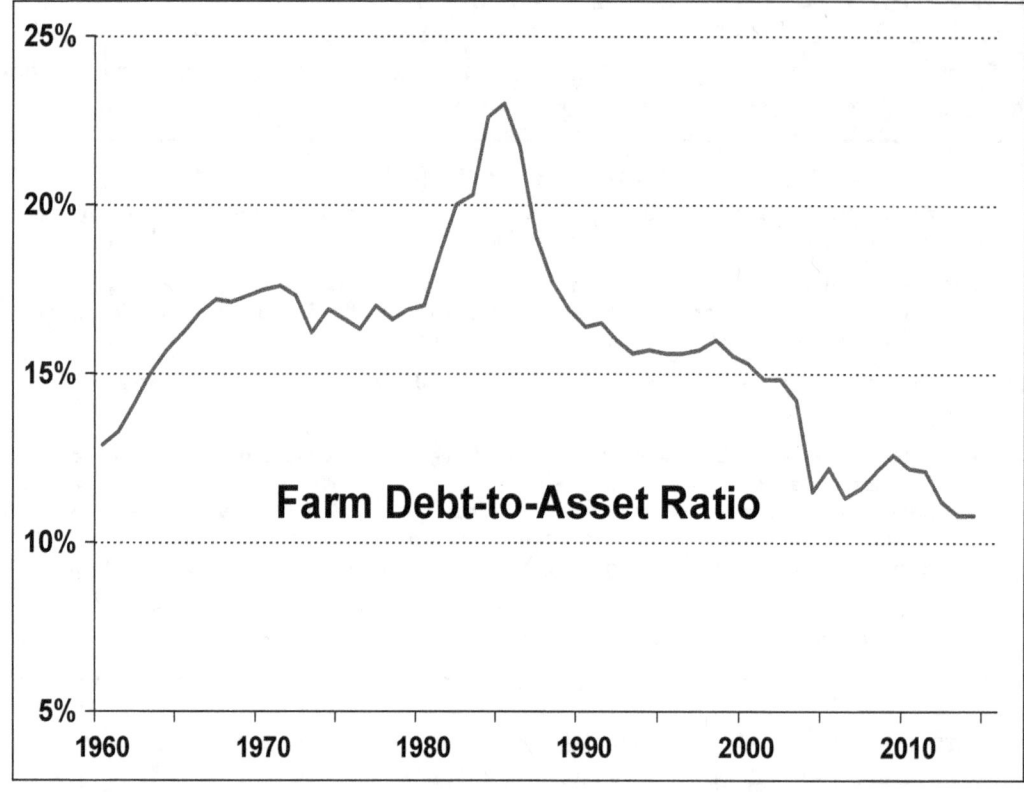

Farm Debt-to-Asset Ratio

Source: USDA, ERS, "2014 Farm Income Forecast," August 26, 2014; 2013 is preliminary, 2014 is forecast

Average Farm Household Income

Farm household wealth is derived from a variety of sources.[13] A farm can have both an on-farm and an off-farm component to its balance sheet of assets and debt. Thus, the well-being of farm operator households is not equivalent to the financial performance of the farm sector or of farm businesses because there are other stakeholders in farming, such as landlords and contractors, and because farm operator households often have nonfarm investments, jobs, and other links to the nonfarm economy.

On-Farm vs. Off-Farm Income Shares

- Average farm household income (sum of on- and off-farm income) is projected at $116,557 (down 2%) in 2014 (**Table 5**).

- The share of farm income derived from off-farm sources had increased steadily for decades but peaked at about 95% in 2002. In 2013, off-farm income is forecasted to account for 81% of the national average farm household income, compared with 19% from farming activities (**Figure 28**).

---

[13] USDA, ERS, "Farm Household Well-being," online webpage accessed on February 28, 2014, at http://www.ers.usda.gov/topics/farm-economy/farm-household-well-being.aspx.

Figure 28. U.S. Average Farm Household Income, by Source, Since 1960

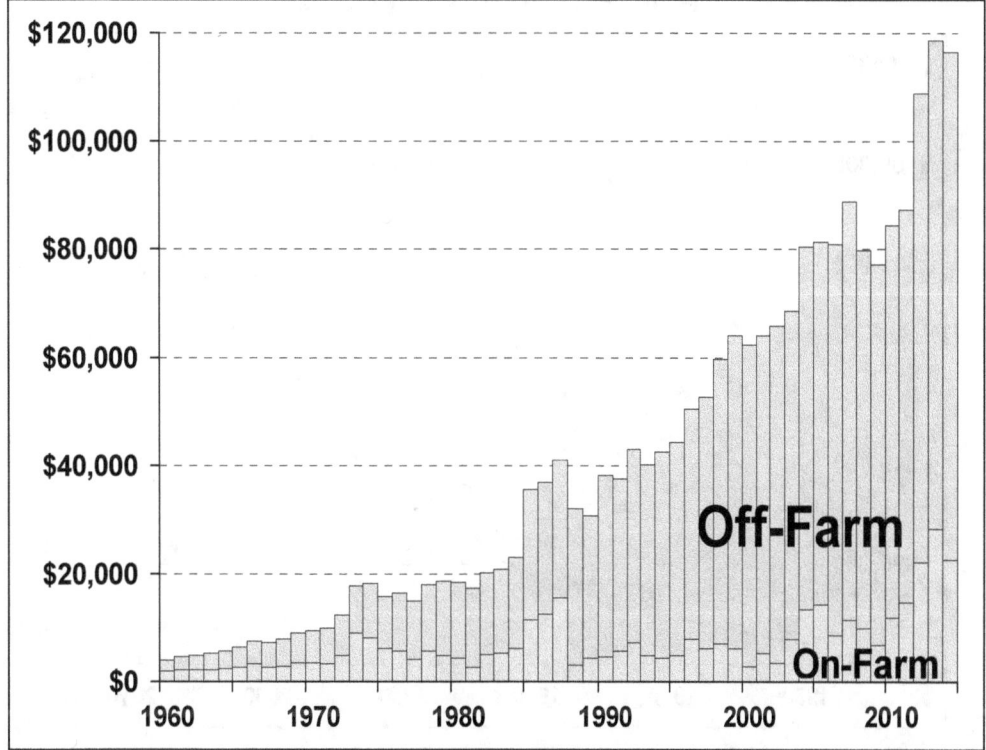

Source: USDA, ERS, "Farm Household Economics and Well-Being: Historic Data On Farm Operator Household Income," November 26, 2013.

U.S. Total vs. Farm Household Average Income

- Since the late 1990s, farm household incomes have surged ahead of average U.S. household incomes (**Figure 29** and **Figure 30**).

- In 2012 (the last year for which comparable data were available), the average farm household income of $108,844 was about 53% higher than the average U.S. household income of $71,274 (**Table 5**).

Figure 29. U.S. Farm Household Incomes Have Surged Well Above Average Household Income Since 1996

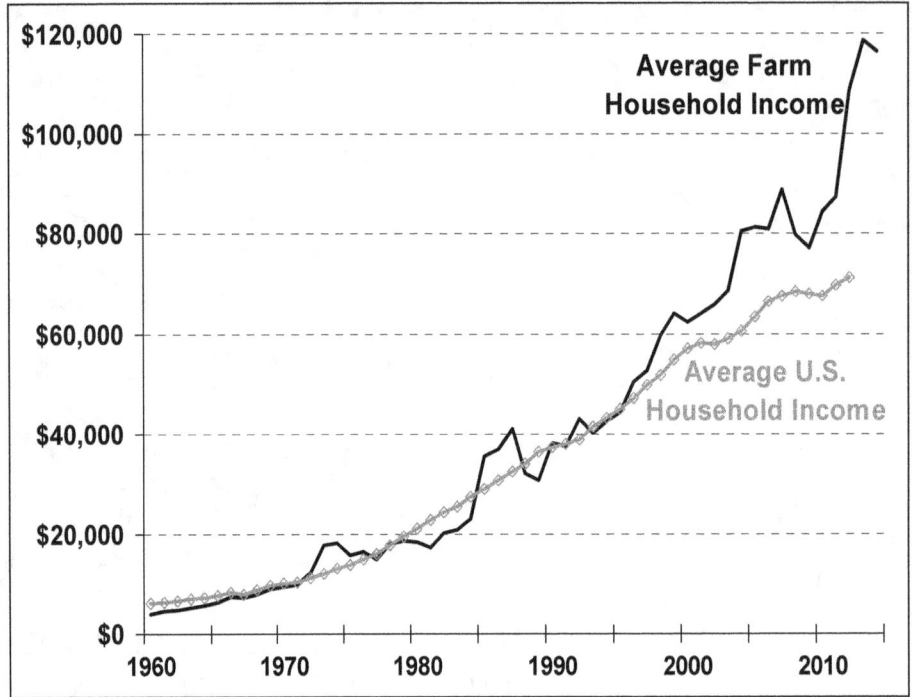

Source: USDA, ERS, "2013 Farm Income Forecast," August 28, 20134.

Note: 2012 is preliminary, 2013 is forecast.

Figure 30. U.S. Farm vs. Average Household Incomes Expressed as a Ratio

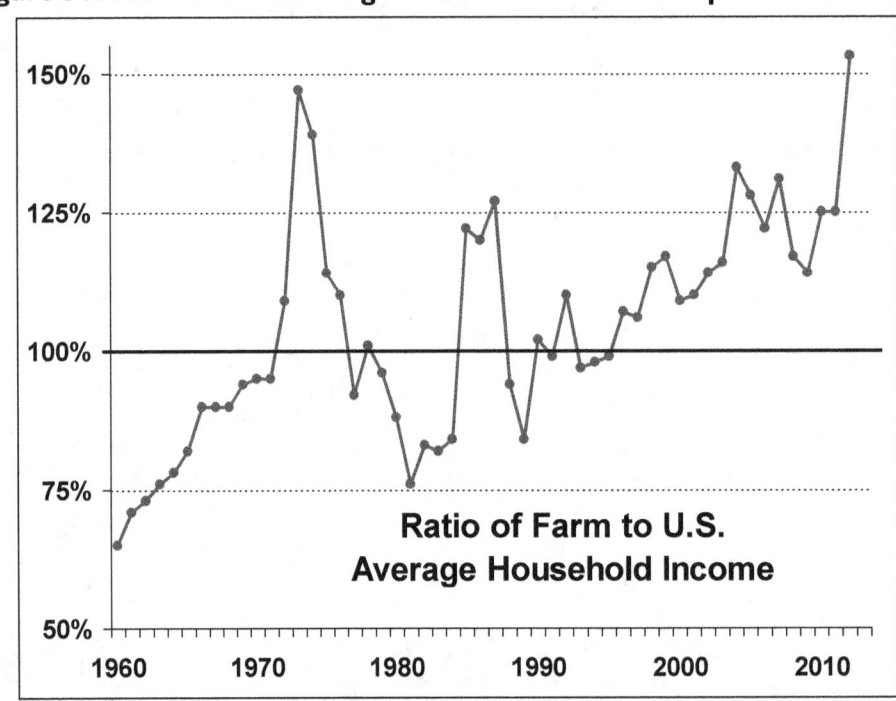

Source: See above source note. 2012 is the last year with comparable data.

Farm Household Income by Sales Class

The share of income from farming increases with farm size as measured by gross sales (**Table 1**).

- "Large" commercial farm households (farms with annual sales greater than $250,000) obtained nearly 75% of household income on-farm and accounted for 82% of the value of total U.S. agricultural production in 2011, while representing only about 10% of farm households.[14]

- Intermediate family farms (farms with annual sales in excess of $10,000 but less than $250,000) obtained about 10% of household income from on-farm sources, accounted for about 17% of the value of total U.S. agricultural production, and represented about 30% of family farms.

- "Small" farm households (annual sales ≤ $10,000) actually lost revenue from farm operations (-9% of household income) and accounted for slightly more than 1% of the value of total U.S. agricultural production in 2011, while representing 59% of farm households. Many of these small farms are classified as rural residence farms and either receive little or no income from farm sources or have a total income level that qualifies them as limited-resource farms.

Table 1. Distribution of Farms and Value of Production by Gross Farm Sales, 2011

| Value of Gross Sales | Family Farms | | Total U.S. Production | Total Household Income (Mean) | | |
	Number	Share	Share	On-farm Share	Off-farm Share	Total Value
< $10,000	1,255,816	59%	1.2%	-9%	109%	$70,507
$10,000 to $249,999	639,430	30%	16.5%	10%	90%	$79,780
≥ $250,000	219,422	10%	82.3%	75%	25%	$205,215
All	2,114,668	100%	100.0%	17%	83%	$87,289

Source: USDA, ERS, *Farm Income and Wealth Statistics*; Farm Household Income and Characteristics, updated as of November 27, 2012.

---

[14] For more information on farm typology, see the ERS Briefing Room, *Farm Household Well-Being*, at http://www.ers.usda.gov/topics/farm-economy/farm-household-well-being.aspx.

Table 2. U.S. Crop and Livestock Revenue by Source, 2008-2014F

($ billions)

Item	2009	2010	2011	2012	2013[a]	2014[a]	Change (%)	Share[b] (%)
Field crops	104.8	113.0	131.9	150.2	137.6	122.9	-10.7%	27.1%
Food grains	14.8	14.1	16.8	18.2	16.2	15.7	-3.3%	3.5%
Wheat	11.7	11.1	13.9	15.3	13.4	12.3	-8.2%	2.7%
Rice	3.0	3.0	2.9	2.8	2.8	3.3	19.7%	0.7%
Feed crops	50.5	54.8	72.0	79.1	72.5	60.2	-17.0%	13.3%
Corn	42.5	47.2	62.9	69.2	61.2	48.4	-20.9%	10.7%
Other Grains	2.4	2.3	2.1	2.6	2.7	2.3	-15.0%	0.8%
Hay	5.6	5.3	7.0	7.3	8.6	9.4	10.0%	2.1%
Oil Crops	35.6	36.5	35.6	44.3	42.8	40.5	-5.5%	8.9%
Soybeans	33.7	34.5	33.3	40.7	40.7	38.9	-4.2%	8.6%
Peanuts	0.8	0.9	1.2	2.3	1.6	1.0	-37.9%	0.2%
Cotton (lint & seed)	4.0	7.6	7.4	8.6	6.0	6.6	9.6%	1.5%
Other Crops	64.0	66.6	70.2	73.3	78.5	78.0	-0.6%	17.2%
Fruits and nuts	19.3	21.7	24.4	26.1	27.6	25.3	-8.2%	5.6%
Vegetables	20.4	20.2	20.7	20.6	23.0	22.7	-1.2%	5.0%
All other crops	24.3	24.6	25.0	26.6	28.0	30.0	7.3%	6.6%
Total Crops	168.8	179.5	202.0	223.5	216.1	200.9	-7.0%	44.3%
Meat animals	59.0	69.5	84.7	90.1	92.1	107.2	16.5%	23.7%
Cattle & calves	43.8	51.5	63.0	67.9	68.9	79.5	15.3%	17.5%
Hogs	14.7	18.0	21.8	22.2	23.1	27.7	19.9%	6.1%
Poultry and eggs	32.5	35.5	36.2	39.0	43.7	47.3	8.2%	10.4%
Broilers	21.8	23.7	23.0	24.8	30.0	32.0	6.7%	7.1%
Turkeys	3.6	4.4	5.0	5.4	4.9	5.2	6.6%	1.2%
Eggs	6.1	6.5	7.3	7.8	8.7	10.0	14.2%	2.2%
All dairy	24.3	31.4	39.5	37.0	40.1	48.5	21.0%	10.7%
Other livestock [c]	4.5	5.1	5.5	5.4	5.9	6.5	10.6%	1.4%
Total Livestock	120.3	141.4	165.9	171.6	181.8	209.6	15.3%	46.3%
Government payments	12.2	12.4	10.4	10.6	11.0	9.3	-15.1%	2.1%
Other farm income [d]	22.0	18.3	26.1	33.6	37.1	33.3	-10.4%	7.3%
Total Farm Revenue	323.3	351.7	404.5	439.3	446.1	453.1	1.6%	100%

Source: "USDA, ERS, *Farm Income and Wealth Statistics*"; updated as of August 26, 2014.

a.   Forecast. Change represents year-to-year projected change between 2014 and 2013.

b.   Share of Total Farm Revenue; values are calculated based on 2014 forecasts.

c.   Includes aquaculture, honey, horses and mules, mohair, wool, pelts, and all other livestock products.

d.   Machine hire, custom work, forest products sales, insurance indemnities, and other farm income.

Table 3. U.S. Farm Production Expenses by Source, 2008-2014F

($ billions)

Item	2009	2010	2011	2012	2013[a]	2014[a]	Change[b] (%)	Share[c] (%)
Farm origin inputs	77.3	81.4	94.2	102.9	108.3	112.9	4.3%	34.4%
Feed	45.0	45.4	54.6	59.1	62.4	60.8	-2.7%	18.5%
Livestock	16.7	19.6	21.7	23.4	23.9	29.3	22.6%	8.9%
Seed	15.5	16.3	17.8	20.3	21.9	22.9	4.3%	7.0%
Manufactured inputs	49.0	49.6	57.5	63.2	65.0	67.5	3.9%	20.6%
Fertilizer & lime	20.1	21.0	25.1	28.5	28.3	29.3	3.2%	8.9%
Fuels & oils	12.7	13.2	15.6	15.7	16.6	17.7	6.1%	5.4%
Electricity	4.6	4.6	4.9	5.3	5.4	5.6	3.2%	1.7%
Pesticides	11.5	10.7	11.8	13.7	14.6	15.0	2.8%	4.6%
Other operating expenses	63.2	61.3	65.9	70.4	70.8	75.8	7.0%	23.1%
Repair & maintenance	14.7	14.8	15.5	16.6	17.2	18.3	6.2%	5.6%
Contract labor	3.9	3.9	4.5	4.3	5.0	4.9	-0.6%	1.5%
Machine & Custom work	3.9	4.3	4.0	4.8	4.9	5.2	6.4%	1.6%
Marketing, storage, etc.	10.3	10.3	10.2	10.1	9.4	10.5	11.6%	3.2%
Miscellaneous	30.4	28.0	31.8	34.6	34.4	36.9	7.3%	11.2%
Total Purchased Inputs[d]	189.4	192.3	217.6	236.5	244.1	256.3	5.0%	78.0%
Interest	17.6	16.9	16.0	16.1	17.1	17.9	4.3%	5.4%
Hired Labor	25.0	23.5	22.3	26.6	27.2	28.6	5.1%	8.7%
Property Taxes	8.9	9.3	9.8	10.0	10.3	10.5	1.9%	3.2%
Net Rent to Non-Op. Landlords	9.8	12.6	12.5	15.5	16.2	15.3	-5.7%	4.6%
Total Cash Expenses	249.7	253.9	277.7	304.9	315.3	328.6	4.2%	100%
Capital Consumption	30.1	30.7	32.1	34.2	37.1	37.6	1.5%	
Other Non-Cash expenses	3.5	2.8	2.7	2.0	1.9	2.2	12.1%	
Total Production Expenses	283.0	287.5	312.5	341.1	354.3	368.4	4.0%	

Source: Compiled by CRS from USDA, ERS, *Farm Income and Wealth Statistics*; updated as of August 26, 2014; available at http://www.ers.usda.gov/data-products/farm-income-and-wealth-statistics.aspx.

a. USDA Forecast.

b. Change represents year-to-year projected change between 2014 and 2013.

c. Share of Total Cash Expenses.

d. Sum of farm origin inputs, manufactured inputs, and other operating expenses

Table 4. Annual U.S. Farm Income Since 2007
($ billions)

Item	2007	2008	2009	2010	2011	2012	2013[a]	2014[a]	Change (%)
1. Cash receipts	288.5	316.4	289.1	321.0	367.9	395.1	397.9	410.5	3.2%
Crops[b]	150.1	174.8	168.9	179.5	202.0	223.5	216.1	200.9	-7.0%
Livestock	138.5	141.6	120.3	141.4	165.9	171.6	181.6	209.6	15.3%
2. Government payments[c]	11.9	12.2	12.2	12.4	10.4	10.6	11.0	9.3	-15.1%
Fixed direct payments[d]	5.1	5.1	4.7	4.8	4.7	4.7	4.3	0.7	-85.0%
CCP[e]	1.1	0.7	1.2	0.2	0.0	0.0	0.0	0.0	0.0%
Marketing Loan Benefits[f]	1.1	0.3	1.1	0.1	0.0	0.0	0.0	0.2	0.0%
Conservation	3.1	3.2	2.8	3.5	3.7	3.7	3.7	3.7	-0.1%
Ad hoc and emergency	0.5	2.1	0.6	3.1	1.3	1.1	1.9	3.9	99.7%
All other[g]	1.0	0.8	1.7	0.7	0.7	1.1	0.9	0.6	-28.1%
3. Farm-related income[h]	17.6	21.5	22.0	18.3	26.1	33.6	37.1	33.3	-10.4%
4. Gross cash income (1+2+3)	318.0	350.1	323.3	351.7	404.5	439.3	446.1	451.6	1.3%
5. Cash expenses[i]	240.6	261.1	249.4	253.9	277.7	304.9	315.3	328.6	4.2%
6. NET CASH INCOME	77.4	88.9	73.9	97.7	126.8	134.4	130.8	123.0	-5.9%
7. Total gross revenues[j]	339.6	377.9	343.3	365.5	430.5	454.9	485.6	481.7	-0.8%
8. Total production expenses[k]	269.5	292.6	283.0	287.5	312.5	341.1	354.3	368.4	4.0%
9. NET FARM INCOME	70.0	85.0	60.4	78.0	118.0	113.8	131.3	113.2	-13.8%

Source: USDA, ERS, *Farm Income and Wealth Statistics*; U.S. and State Farm Income and Wealth Statistics, updated as of August 26, 2014.

a. Data for 2013 and 2014 are USDA forecasts. Change represents year-to-year projected change between 2014 and 2013.

b. Includes Commodity Credit Corporation loans under the farm commodity support program.

c. Government payments reflect payments made directly to all recipients in the farm sector, including landlords. The non-operator landlords' share is offset by its inclusion in rental expenses paid to these landlords and thus is not reflected in net farm income or net cash income.

d. Direct payments include production flexibility payments of the 1996 Farm Act through 2001, and fixed direct payments under the 2002 Farm Act since 2002.

e. CCP = counter-cyclical payments.

f. Includes loan deficiency payments (LDP); marketing loan gains (MLG); and commodity certificate exchange gains.

g. Peanut quota buyout, milk income loss payments, and other miscellaneous program payments.

h. Income from custom work, machine hire, agri-tourism, forest product sales, and other farm sources.

i. Excludes depreciation and perquisites to hired labor.

j. Gross cash income plus inventory adjustments, the value of home consumption, and the imputed rental value of operator dwellings.

k. Cash expenses plus depreciation and perquisites to hired labor.

Table 5. Average Annual Income per U.S. Household, Farm versus All, 2006-2013F

($ per household)

	2007	2008	2009	2010	2011	2012	2013F	2014F
Average U.S. Farm Income by Source								
On-Farm Income	$11,364	$9,764	$6,866	$11,788	$14,625	$22,087	$28,223	$22,629
Off-Farm income	$77,432	$70,032	$70,302	$72,671	$72,665	$86,757	$89,377	$93,928
Total Farm income	$88,796	$79,796	$77,169	$84,459	$87,290	$108,844	$118,699	$116,557
Average U.S. Household Income	$67,609	$68,424	$67,976	$67,530	$69,677	$71,274	na	na
Farm Household Income as Share of U.S. Avg. Household Income (%)	131%	117%	114%	125%	125%	153%	na	na

Source: USDA, ERS, *Farm Household Income and Characteristics*, principal farm operator household finances, data set updated as of August 26, 2014; at http://www.ers.usda.gov/data-products/farm-household-income-and-characteristics.aspx.

Note: Data for 2012 and 2013 are USDA forecasts.

Table 6. Average Annual Farm Sector Debt-to-Asset Ratio, 2006-2014F

($ billions)

	2007	2008	2009	2010	2011F	2012	2013P	2014F
Farm Assets	2,077.4	2,154.0	2,131.5	2,294.5	2,433.5	2,689.6	2,839.9	2,906.3
Farm Debt	240.7	261.1	268.3	278.9	294.5	300.3	305.3	313.5
Farm Equity	1,841.2	1,893.0	1,863.1	2,015.6	2,139.0	2,389.3	2,534.6	2,592.8
Debt-to-Asset Ratio (%)	**11.6%**	**12.1%**	**12.6%**	**12.2%**	**12.1%**	**11.2%**	**10.8%**	**10.8%**

Source: USDA, ERS, *Farm Income and Wealth Statistics*; U.S. and State Farm Income and Wealth Statistics, updated as of August 26, 2014; available at http://www.ers.usda.gov/data-products/farm-income-and-wealth-statistics.aspx.

Note: Data for 2013 are preliminary, 2014 are USDA forecasts.

Table 7. U.S. Prices and Support Rates for Selected Farm Commodities Since 2008/09 Marketing Year

Commodity[a]	Unit	Year	2009/10	2010/11	2011/12	2012/13	2013/14	2014/15F[b]	% change from 2013/14[c]	2015/16P[b]	% change from 2014/15[d]	2014 Loan Rate[e]	2014 Reference Price
Wheat	$/bu	Jun-May	4.87	5.70	7.24	7.77	6.87	5.80-6.80	-8.3%	—	—	2.94	5.50
Corn	$/bu	Sep-Aug	3.55	5.18	6.22	6.89	4.40-4.50	3.55-4.25	-12.4%	—	—	1.95	3.70
Sorghum	$/bu	Sep-Aug	3.22	5.02	5.99	6.33	4.20-4.30	3.30-4.00	-14.1%	—	—	1.95	3.95
Barley	$/bu	Jun-May	4.66	3.86	5.35	6.43	6.06	4.35-5.15	-21.6%	—	—	1.85	4.95
Oats	$/bu	Jun-May	2.02	2.52	3.49	3.89	3.75	2.65-3.25	-21.3%	—	—	1.33	2.40
Rice	$/cwt	Aug-Jul	14.40	12.70	14.50	15.10	15.90	13.80-14.80	-10.1%	—	—	6.50	14.00
Soybeans	$/bu	Sep-Aug	9.59	11.30	12.50	14.40	13.00	9.35-11.35	-20.4%	—	—	5.00	8.40
Soybean oil	¢/lb	Oct-Sep	35.95	53.20	51.90	47.13	38.50	35-39	-42.9%	—	—	—	—
Soybean meal	$/st	Oct-Sep	311.27	345.52	393.53	468.11	470.0	340-380	-23.4%	—	—	—	—
Cotton, Upland	¢/lb	Aug-Jul	62.9	81.50	88.3	72.5	77.5	58-72	-16.1%	—	—	47 - 52	none
Choice Steers	$/cwt	Jan-Dec	83.25	95.38	114.73	122.86	125.89	150-153	20.3%	149-162	2.6%	—	—
Barrows/Gilts	$/cwt	Jan-Dec	41.24	55.06	66.11	60.88	64.05	79-81	24.9%	72-78	-6.3%	—	—
Broilers	¢/lb	Jan-Dec	77.60	82.90	79.0	86.6	99.7	103-106	4.8%	100-108	-0.5%	—	—
Eggs	¢/doz	Jan-Dec	103.0	106.30	115.3	117.4	124.7	136-139	10.3%	124-134	-6.2%	—	—
Milk	$/cwt	Jan-Dec	12.83	16.26	20.14	18.53	20.05	23.55-23.75	18.0%	19.75-20.75	-14.4%	—	—

Source: Various USDA agency sources as described in the notes below.

a. Season average farm price for grains and oilseeds are from USDA, National Agricultural Statistical Service, *Agricultural Prices*. Calendar year data are for the first year, for example, 2000/2001 = 2000; F = forecast and P = projection from *World Agricultural Supply and Demand Estimates* (WASDE) August 12, 2014; — = no value; and USDA's out-year 2015/2016 crop price forecasts will first appear in the May 2015 WASDE report. Soybean and livestock product prices are from USDA, Agricultural Marketing Service (AMS): soybean oil—Decatur, IL, cash price, simple avg. crude; soybean meal—Decatur, IL, cash price, simple avg. 48% protein; choice steers—Nebraska, direct 1100-1300 lbs.; barrows/gilts—national base, live equivalent 51%-52% lean; broilers—wholesale, 12-city avg.; eggs—Grade A, New York, volume buyers; and milk—simple avg. of prices received by farmers for all milk.

b. Data for 2014/2015 are USDA forecasts; 2015/2016 data are USDA projections.

c. Percent change from 2013/2014, calculated using the difference from the midpoint of the range for 2014/2015 with the estimate for 2013/2014.

d. Percent change from 2014/2015, calculated using the difference from the midpoint of the range for 2015/2016 with the estimate for 2014/2015.

e. Loan rate and reference prices are for the 2014/2015 crop year. See CRS Report R43076, *The 2014 Farm Bill (P.L. 113-79): Summary and Side-by-Side*.

Author Contact Information

Randy Schnepf
Specialist in Agricultural Policy
rschnepf@crs.loc.gov, 7-4277